# USING COMPUTERS TO CREATE ART

# USING COMPUTERS TO CREATE ART

## Implications for Artists and Art Educators

Tracey Bowen

The Edwin Mellen Press
Lewiston•Queenston•Lampeter

**Library of Congress Cataloging-in-Publication Data**

Bowen, Tracey
Using computers to create art : implications for artists and art educators / Tracey Bowen
p. cm.
Includes bibliographical references and index.
ISBN-13: 978-0-7734-5655-6
ISBN-10: 0-7734-5655-4
1. Art and computers. 2. Human-computer interaction. I. Title.

N72.C63B69 2006
702.85--dc22

2006050413

*hors série.*

A CIP catalog record for this book is available from the British Library.

*Front cover: Mixed media and digital print by Tracey Bowen*
*Author photo by Rebecca Bowen*



The Edwin Mellen Press
Box 450
Lewiston, New York
USA 14092-0450

The Edwin Mellen Press
Box 67
Queenston, Ontario
CANADA L0S 1L0

The Edwin Mellen Press, Ltd.
Lampeter, Ceredigion, Wales
UNITED KINGDOM SA48 8LT

Printed in the United States of America

This book is dedicated to William and Elizabeth Thomas, my loving and supportive parents.

**Table of Contents**

## Foreword

With the recent addition of the computer to the realm of art making and production, artists, art theorists and historians, and art educators have pondered how to meaningfully incorporate and articulate the presence of the digital newcomer. Tracey Bowen tackles this question straight on in her timely and salient study about cyborgs in the studio making art by hand and computer. Bowen's work, initially autobiographical because of her artistic struggle to understand how incorporating the computer has altered her art making by hand, examines the dialectic and gaps resulting from the often dichotomizing effects of the computer, the mouse, the Internet, and differing software applications on a particular group of artists as they merge computers with their traditional modes of art making such as drawing and painting. She does so through clear elaboration of the theoretical spaces she enters and crosses, and particularly through micro case studies of six practicing artists at differing stages of computer incorporation. Central to the project are the six case studies employing qualitative field face-to-face interview and ethnographic observation to bring forward the artists' voices.

Bowen's exploration is at the same time historical, noting debates and problematics with the addition of computer technologies to the realm of art making so clearly illuminated in the six artist interview narratives, and visionary in her meaningful offerings of the hybrid cyborg artist, cyborg vocabulary for artists, and cyborg pedagogy that can be employed in arts education and beyond. Often in the articulations of the world of the digital and its relationships to the visual arts, the rhetoric finds a more abstract plateau where debates among theorists leave us with abstract formulations of the interconnections of these differing worlds. The recent gathering of the First International Conference on the Histories of New Media, Science, and Technology at Banff, Alberta in September 2005 well illustrates this problem for abstract debate centered on whether or not the history of new media arts was related to what is labeled as the History of Art, with many delegates vowing strongly that there was little relationship. Bowen, grounded in theory and astutely situating herself within the overarching spaces of visual culture resonating the writings of Nicholas Mirzoeff, does quite the opposite. She pursues her exploration through the living and working of six practicing artists who struggle with incorporating the computer into their hand made art making conceptualizations and practices. Her investigative process is one that is transparent, getting "inside the skin" of the six artists and enabling their voices to illuminate their struggles in the interlinking of the computer and their hand made processes.

Unusual in the study is the array of angles that Bowen takes in working as a theorist, practicing artist, and art educator. Convincingly and with ease she crosses back and forth in trans-disciplinary and inter-disciplinary shifts that enable the capturing and relational interconnecting of the broad spaces of theory, artist, art education, and the realm of the digital. In teasing out themes and patterns in the six artists' interview stories she focuses on a key component across narratives of the act of translating between manual and digital modes of art making; Bowen pursues what can be gleaned from the gaps in between.

Her pursuit leads to a rich inventive space, re-purposing the gaps in re-conceptualizing and re-imagining the collaboration between hand working abilities and computer technologies in a new community of hybrid art practitioners. The now legendary work of Donna Haraway in her theoretical development of the cyborg grounds Bowen's new community, articulating both epistemological and political stances for using technologies to develop connections with each other, the life world, and the world of the arts. It gives place and connection to the hand making art producer in the human/machine interface, and moves beyond the domains of the traditional and modern art spheres in which the drawer and painter often find themselves.

Bowen's pursuit moves on to an initial development of a cyborg vocabulary for artists. The computer is no longer viewed as a "tool" or as something that is distanced from the body; it becomes a co-maker of images in a new interactive spatial relationship comprised of a fluid network of exchanges.

The concept of coupling or couplet is key to her emergent vocabulary, in which the cyborg has the potential to produce fruitful and meaningful couplings of human/machine relationships and complementarities.

The realm of the cyborg has much to offer in what Bowen labels "cyborg pedagogy," bringing forward a conceptual space for an educative critique of the interconnectedness of the body and technology. The idea of digital espistemologies opens up new ways of knowing about the interlinking of old and new art making media. Cyborg pedagogy provides a vehicle through which to challenge assumptions, to question imposed dominant narratives, and to give artists opportunities to critique the influences of digital technologies on their work. Bowen's conceptualization of "cyborg pedagogy" offers the field of Art Education, in its workings with computer technologies and the visual arts, a way to move beyond the field bound parameters it often places around itself.

In considering the realms of hand art making and the digital which remain conceptually and relationally problematic, Bowen provides a refreshing approach in which she searches out and investigates the dialectic and the gaps from the vantage point of moving relationships and our knowledge of them forward. In grappling with making art by hand and by computer, her cyborgs in the studio do just that.

Mary Leigh Morbey
Associate Professor of Culture and Technology
Associate Director of the Institute for Research on Learning Technologies
York University, Toronto

## Acknowledgments

Looking back on the journey that has led to the completion of this book, I see that the process has been similar to preparing for, and running a race. While I may be the one to actually "run" the race, it is only through the help of many others like coaches, trainers, supporters, care givers and other competitors that I can get to the finish line. Therefore, I would like to thank those individuals. I thank the many artists who have influenced my thinking and inspired me to undergo this exploration, especially those who participated in the study. Your voices in particular add such texture and impetus to my endeavour. I would like to thank Robert Morgan for his tireless support of my work, his thorough attention to detail and his "coaching" that has empowered me to cross the finish line. I am indebted to his contribution. I would also like to thank Mary Leigh Morbey who opened up my thinking about cultural production in a wired world and has mentored me in my research endeavours. I also thank my many friends and colleagues who have listened to my thoughts, ideas, worries and obsessions throughout this journey. Lastly, I would like to thank my parents and my family. They have been supportive of all that I have set out to do. My two daughters, Kathryn and Rebecca, have not only been patient with me, they have also become colleagues as we exchange our "writing woes" and listen to each other's ideas. I wish them well as they start new journeys of their own. And to my partner and soul mate, Bob, thank you for coming along this journey with me and cheering me on to the finish.

# INTRODUCTION

For centuries artists have manipulated tools and materials in the service of creative activity and the "making" of art objects and images. The creative process has enabled individuals to develop autonomy through self expression and the mastery of skills. The computer age, however, has complicated and challenged artist' work in many ways. Collaborative engagements using the "computer machine" challenges autonomy, reconstitutes the mastery of skills, and questions materiality across a variety of "reality statuses" (Morse, 1995).

The questions that inspired this book developed out of changes to my own art practice and my reflections about the impact of "the machine" on creative activity and self expression. I began to question what I had to say about the changing environment and where I fit as an artist. What happens to artistic integrity and my autonomy as a creator when the resulting vision is not necessarily all mine? Furthermore, how would this collaborative work be perceived and valued by others who privilege "original" art? If I was unsettled about the role of computer technology within my art making processes others might be as well. The tensions created by these questions are not necessarily resolvable.

This book is a way of working through and understanding how making art in a digital culture means that artists must live with tension and contradiction as driving forces that contribute to their creative processes and new ways of interpreting the world around them. This book includes six micro case studies that are enveloped within a broader inquiry and discussion into the integration of computers within art making practice. The artists' stories that emerge from the case studies provide a context for exploring how manual and digital ways of working are becoming more integrated across many different forms of everyday routines. The individual stories that unfold across the next few chapters, particularly chapters 3 and 4, explore in depth the issues I have described, and culminate in a discussion of emerging theories and broader pedagogical implications of understanding the relations of interchange and exchange across manual and digital procedures for producing imagery within the latter chapters.

The specific organization of the entire research project that comprises this book is structured in the following manner. Chapter 1 contextualizes the study within visual arts practice and explores the current cultural climate whereby computerization of everyday living and working practices has also moved into the art making studio. Chapter 1 also introduces the reader to the need for research and inquiry into artists' changing working and thinking processes in a digital age.

Chapter 2 presents a set of conceptual lenses that prompt a rethinking of art making as artists move across both physical and virtual domains while developing ideas and producing imagery. The lenses have been developed using current literature across varied discourses, including those concerned with art education. Most of the available literature looks at computer use through and within the discipline of art education, but it does not address artists who are trying to integrate manual and digital processes in their studios without the support of an outside educational institution. Important to this discussion are the ways in which "the studio" is perceived as a place for producing images and how these perceptions are historically and socially constructed. Specific to these issues are the ways in which artists negotiate older and newer modes of art making within these historical and social constructions. This is particularly useful for placing the six artists' experiences along a continuum that needs more intense examination.

Chapter 3 presents the six artists who participated in the micro case studies and begins to examine and analyze their stories that emerged from the face-to-face interviews. The six artists are all in various stages of integrating computer use within their primarily manual art making practices. The artists responded to a set of questions regarding their own art making and Web navigating practices as well as how they perceived their hand-making is affected by digital technologies. The artists describe how they integrate computer programs into their art making procedures and explain how they feel they are benefiting from these new explorations and what they feel is at stake because of computerization. Common themes and threads are excavated, discussed and interpreted in relation to the larger questions posed by the research. As well, new issues initiated by the artists' translations of working by hand and then by computer are explored in relation to the crossover phenomenon that emerges from their dialogue. The artists' stories are the fundamental data for interpreting the relation of theory and practice as they grapple with new media technologies and develop new aspects of their artist-selves through auto poiēsis.

Chapter 4 elaborates on the artists' conversations excavating three particular themes that describe online researching in relation to art and image production, computerized production of art and imagery, and the physical and virtual spaces of making. Similarities and differences among the artists' descriptions are highlighted and explored in relation to the varied ways in which they are integrating computers into their practices and the crossovers between manual and digital processes they are negotiating. The artists move between the two domains both comfortably and anxiously at various points in their art making. Interwoven with the artists' stories are a variety of theoretical discourses including those concerned with philosophical perspectives of technology, globalization, aporias, information access and excess, aesthetics and anaesthetics and cinematic hapticity. These theories inform my process of deconstructing the artists' accounts of their negotiations across physical and virtual terrains for making art.

Chapter 5 examines issues of space and place as they are related to making art by hand and by computer. I explore the crossover phenomenon inherent in the ways the artists work across differences in conditions, often translating their procedures within three particular spatial realms. The three realms examined here are haptical space, narrative space, and paradoxical space. The places and spaces for making art become problematized when artists work concurrently across both physical and virtual environments in developing and producing imagery.

Chapter 6 examines the possibilities that open up for artists who are using their home computers to reconceptualize and re-imagine their hand working abilities in different ways. They are becoming a new community of hybrid art practitioners. These artists are exploring joint kinships with their computers in order to realize new ways of working and being. The chapter also focuses on the possibilities of the cyborg identity as a way of becoming via Donna Haraway's cyborg manifesto, and the need for a new cyborg vocabulary to describe making by hand and computer together.

Chapter 7 addresses the implications of the research findings and the emergent theories presented in relation to artists' practices and the changing role of art education and the teaching studio in digital cultures. Areas for further research are outlined and the chapter concludes with thoughts on my own art practice and how I have been affected by this entire research process.

My work then is the result of a strong desire to understand how art making practice is affected by media forms such as digital image manipulation programs, the Internet and the Web, and to find new intersections between theory and practice. This research opens up the study of both handmade and computer assisted creative processes and their potential to inform each other pedagogically.

The significance of the artists' stories in relation to human/computer interface research may vary from reader to reader. Practicing artists may be interested in the translations of practical techniques and approaches to creating imagery while art history scholars may be asking more questions about the impact of technology and the ways in which artists develop hybrid forms of representation and communication over time. Nonetheless, readers are invited to reconsider their own relationships to computers and how computerized negotiations influence their explorations of the world. Furthermore, art educators in particular, are called upon to reconsider what is happening within their classrooms as students explore new ways of thinking about old materials and techniques in an effort to become digital in their day to day learning.

# CHAPTER ONE: DISRUPTIONS & DISPLACEMENTS

The computerization of so many daily rituals, routines, and ways of working has, at times, left many individuals who regularly use computers, myself included, feeling dislocated and disrupted from the fixed locale we understood as the ground of our culture. New media and technology advancements have accelerated the pace of daily life and destabilized our relationships to the places where we live and inform ourselves about the world. The ways in which information is received have changed for those of us who engage new information technologies, potentially affecting the ways in which we create meaning. The terms on which we relate to our locale, to the people around us, and to embedded daily rituals have also changed. Those of us experiencing this unfixedness and disruption are continually striving to rework our sense of identity in light of this upheaval. As one's identity has traditionally been "inseparable from a sense of location," the task of relocating oneself in a multitude of new contexts and situations requires a reconceptualization of how to negotiate what was once familiar terrain (Collins 1995:31). Reconceptualization means changing our terms of engagement with the world and its informants.

As a visual artist and former painter, I have felt these disruptions most immediately in the ways that I produce imagery and make art. I have moved from traditional artists' materials such as graphite and paint, to collaborating with a computer driven colour photo-copier. Recalling my initial resistance to working with this machine, I also remember the fervor many years ago when computers began infiltrating the work places of large and small companies. Many of the workers feared that human sensibilities and capabilities were being replaced with machines. I felt a degree of that same dread when I gave over a part of my creative process to the capabilities of the photo-copy machine.

The trepidation continues today. Change is ever-present in the ways we all engage in the "mundane practices that directly contribute to [our] ongoing life-narratives" (Tomlinson 1999:20). Disruptions to the routine practices of daily living and working, and eventual transformations of these practices are due in large part to globalization and what Tomlinson refers to as "complex connectivity" (p.2). Complex connectivity describes the transformations occurring in relation to a "rapidly developing and ever densening network of interconnections and interdependencies" that have become the underpinnings of daily life (p.2). Interconnections and interdependencies have broad implications across many sectors of our existence because they enable us to experience distances and relationships between people and places in new ways.

Representatively, distant places have become much more accessible because of new communications technologies and the ever expanding media presentations. Individuals' experiences become complicated through their connectivity with others on a larger front, putting into question the identities they had been constructing from what they thought was a fixed locale. Computer technologies and the Internet have been two central contributors to complex connectivity (Tomlinson 1999:20). The introduction of computerization into even the most mundane of everyday activities has caused disturbances for a great many people. Artists in particular, are grappling with computers not only in their own everyday activities but, rather more consequentially, in their art making processes and routines.

Ten to fifteen years ago, most artists would not have even considered using a computer as part of their art making process. Computer-assisted imagery was reserved for science fiction or considered the realm of university technology labs like those at MIT. In the art world, as in other sectors of society, computerization caused an upheaval in familiar ways of working and making. A great number of traditionally-based artists, such as painters and those who make drawings, resisted using a computer to produce imagery. Whereas many older artists were slower to approach the computer as a way to facilitate image production, younger artists who grew up using computers in school, have more easily embraced computers in the studio. I count myself as one of those artists, a traditional painter, who initially put up a wall of resistance.

As I began to entertain the idea of using a computer to produce imagery, I found myself collaborating with a new partner, that of a machine. This new collaboration however, was creating a disconcerting rupture in my art making practice. By using the colour photocopier and its computer driven editing system to develop and produce my images, I was becoming emotionally and physically dislocated from the familiarity of my usual choice of media, the fixed painter's canvas. This developed even though I had found a new flexibility that expanded my options for producing images and creating new meanings. The actualization of the rupture occurred when I realized I could not go back to painting. It was not that the new opportunities to create multiples of an image supplanted my need to create a master original as I had formally learned to do as a printmaker. My computerized processes of creating, manipulating and then multiplying original images conceptually echoed the traditional printing procedures I had used in the past. The dislocation came from the machine.

The computer-driven colour photocopier contested my grounded, modernist assumptions and perceptions about making art and being an artist. As Sherry Turkle has suggested, I saw myself much differently when I "caught sight of [my] image in the mirror of the machine" (1995:9). I experienced the dislocation in such a way that, for a time, it destabilized my way of being an artist. The process was not labour intensive, the production of multiples was endless and the object created did not have my physical hand markings embedded in its *thingness*. For me, this raised the issue of how computers were affecting me as well as other artists.

My own experiences of reworking my image production using a

computerized machine have inspired this research. In particular, I am interested in investigating how artists are using their home computers for image and text production. This concern has led to my conversations with six other artists of varying age and career levels who appear to be grappling with the machine like I have, some more easily than others. The artists, mostly painters, have all been acquaintances from some aspect of my own interactions with the art communities of the Toronto and the Hamilton regions. They are all working to create a balance between making art and making a living, a common pursuit among working artists. While all have experienced some degree of commercial success that is not necessarily their motive for art making. They are everyday workers with limited resources. Like a majority of artists in the community, they are unattached to institutions that can provide elaborate digital imaging and computer equipment and programs. This kind of equipment is often unavailable to most artists because of cost and space limitations.

The six artists I invited to participate in my investigation represent many other art makers who, with restricted amounts of time and money, are attempting to integrate the use of home computers into their working processes. They all have stories to tell about how they came to involve computers in their daily lives and then eventually within their art making approaches and procedures. Of particular interest here is what the artists have to say about their art-making practice that straddles manual and digital procedures, and how they are negotiating the space in between as part of their approach to developing ideas. I have deliberately only chosen six artists so I may treat their stories as short case studies that describe their experiences, perceptions, and working habits. The limited number of case studies allows for a more in-depth exploration of the issues at stake. While the stories told throughout this book may not represent all artists' experiences within the digital arena this in-depth exploration of the artists' descriptions of their ways of making in terms of what they highlight, how they feel challenged, and the areas of computer-aided making they resist, is of great benefit to the almost nonexistent literature regarding studio practice. Instead of a wide-ranging survey of many artists, the six micro case studies focus on the commonalities and differences amongst this much smaller, yet diverse group of working professionals.

**Looking at artists who use computers**

My motives for this investigation are to explore how creative procedures used in one context such as manual art making in the physical world, are transferred to the computer world of digital manipulation and cyberspace and then vice versa. The inquiry highlights common traits among the artists in how they accommodate and integrate these crossovers between various media domains. The autobiographical implications of these crossovers are pertinent to the artists' understanding of the underlying "lived curriculum" they are cultivating every day (Grumet 1981:140). To know one's lived curriculum is to see one's life as a course that is followed, rerouted, and reconstituted as new events affect the direction of the course. Autobiography is the underlying condition under which the lived curriculum develops. The artists' actions, both real (physical) and virtual become pedagogical as they provide openings through their own questions. We see their stories of using computers in relation to our own stories and the stories of others.

The research that constitutes this book also offers the opportunity to develop a "cyber-pedagogy" (*cf.* Garoian & Gaudelius, 2001) through a critical reading of how artists negotiate the various areas of cyberspace. The possibilities for new explorations of cultural production in what might begin as unfamiliar territory, opens up alternative pedagogical sites within a diversity of contexts. Integral to developing these opportunities is the process of defining, redefining and reconceptualizing culturally inspired terms and popular practices used across the various discourses that are employed as a framework for this project. My intention is to develop a new vocabulary for hybrid cyber and digital procedures for image production.

The artists that I have invited to tell their stories for this investigation are not unusual in their traditional approaches to making art. Like most other artists, they engage in exploring, questioning, researching and making as ways of developing their practice. However, since our culture is exhibiting an increased reliance on computers and a fascination with the Internet and the World Wide Web (Web), these terms of engagement have become more complex. The Web in itself is a source of an incredible, often overwhelming, sometimes time-wasting, amount of information that can be multidimensional and multi contextual. New cyber cultures and visual languages have been created, offering networks of diverse communities which challenge and influence the traditional ways in which artists have constructed their identities. These challenges are not always welcome. Connectivity is beneficial to those artists who seek out new ways to collaborate on image and art production, yet collaboration can be threatening to others who choose to wear their autonomy as creators like an inviolable shroud.

Turkle's (1995) research concerning the influences of the Internet on identity, including personality shifts between real life and virtual reality, has provided a foundation for some of the psychological and sociological changes in a culture that is "connected" and gives a context for exploring changes the artists have perceived in their own lives. In this transitional phase of digital culture, artists can create a window for looking inward on culture as they interrogate the impact of computer technologies at a "deeper psycho-sensorial level" (De Kerckhove 1995:170). They pose questions about their (and our) identity in relation to technology and how their lives are being affected by the machines. They can be cultural barometers of sorts. The intention of my research is to examine the dialectic resulting from the often dichotomizing effects of new machines on a particular group of artists as they merge computers and communications technologies with their traditional modes of art making such as drawing and painting.

Many artists are now investing in home computers for a variety of reasons such as the administrative details entailed in their career management, or the fast-growing needs of school aged children at home. These artists are beginning to explore ways in which the computer can enhance their own image and text production. These new interventions prompt questions such as how is their art making practice affected by digital manipulation capabilities and the endless information possibilities offered by the Web, and how are they transferring these new approaches of developing ideas to their hands-on, manual forms of art making?

In light of my own struggle with the machine, I am interested in exploring whether the artists that I interviewed recognize the dialogic relationship between their manual selves and their digital selves in their processes. It is through their descriptive stories within our interview conversations that the artists provide the data for addressing these questions. They speak about how they investigate ideas using the Web, the physicality of manifesting those ideas through the hands-on making of art objects, how they have integrated digital processes into their manual approach to art making, how they have adapted to the constant change and innovation offered by digital technologies, and the experiences they recognize as important to shaping their practices. The artists describe their art making practices in relation to how they perceive they have been influenced and affected by digital culture and the use of computers. It is through these descriptions that their individual ways of "being digital" (Negroponte 1995) at different points in their art making processes emerge, adding to the discussion on broader issues regarding human/computer interfaces.

The artists' conversational interviews provide a rich foundation of information to be analyzed and interpreted. I have chosen to limit the study to six artists so that I can focus intensely on the stories told and the language used in each conversation. This intense focus is required for examining the artists' stories in order to see at which points their computer assisted art making processes are both similar and different from the key procedures used in their mark-making, manual processes. Examining which approaches appear to have remained the same and which approaches have changed, illuminate how the artists traverse physical and virtual terrains in the studio. In this way, my investigation uses the artists' stories as part of the larger framing story of how using computers places all of us at the crossroads of two contexts, that of the physical and that of the virtual.

The process of opening up and examining the artists' stories is driven by my own need to understand how new technological and digital environments are affecting the research, development, and working processes of artists, including myself, who make art by hand. This being said, when I first conceived of this project my interest was focused on the visual appearance of the Web and how digitized graphics are affecting the visual sensibilities of myself and other artists. I questioned how our view of the world through the flood of pixilated imagery on a small screen was altering our visual sensibilities and, in turn, being reflected in the images employed for real-world art making. It became apparent, however, that what I would be looking at was the effect of one form of visual representation on another within the larger framework of visual culture (Barnard 1998; Duncum 2001; Farmer 2000; Frieling 1996; Helfand 2001; Landow 2000; Mirzoeff 1998; Sturken & Cartwright 2001). Fine art disciplines, often referred to as High Art (Varnedoe & Gopnik 1990) have been challenged by media such as photography (Barthes 1977; Lalvani 1996; Crary1999) film, (Benjamin 1968; Donald 1999; Krauss 1993; Friedberg1998) and television (Farmer 2000). Computerized imagery and the Web have furthered these challenges (Bruckman1995; Frieling 1996; Gigliotti 2000).

The challenges created by computer imagery to fine art forms such as painting, become less daunting by probing the ways in which different visual representations affect each other through reciprocity. The reciprocity of one form of visual representation on many others is ever increasing. The mutual relationship between film and television through image, screen, and viewer relationships is just one example (Friedberg 1995). These kinds of interdependent relationships are continued by computerization. Software companies and web designers often take up the challenge of digitally recreating the formal properties of traditional painting, drawing, video, etc., including establishing trade names for these new programs like *Paintbrush,* and embedding in these new forms assumptions still related to the older forms (Elkins 2001). This in itself produces both a dialogue and a dichotomy between newer and older forms, placing the user in flux. Some are somewhat suspect, as is the case of the older artists I interviewed for this study. Instead of comparing the visual attributes inherent in the appearance of one media form to another as they are presented on some form of a screen, whether televisual, cinematic, computer or canvas, my investigation focuses on the particular dialogue between manual processes of image and text production and digital possibilities that can enhance or even replace those forms of production. This dialogue emerges as a result of the artists' descriptions of their ways of making art. The dialectic develops when an artist approaches art making from a traditional *manual-creator self* as well as from an emergent digital self and has prompted my further exploration into the artists' "hands-on" engagement with traditional mark-making materials in relation to their experiences with digital manipulation of images using a computer mouse. At issue here are the artists' various comfort levels of working by hand and by mouse.

The aesthetic sensibilities of "handmade" art versus the production of computer-assisted imagery, along with related formal concerns of colour, depth, texture, composition and visual appeal, are indeed important to this discussion, integral to how the artists see themselves and the rest of the world through imagery produced across diverse sites within visual culture. However, the focus of this particular study is the way in which a small group of artists is integrating digital procedures with their manual ways of producing imagery and art, insofar as these relations of integration are prompting new hybrid ways of working that demand closer investigation and new vocabularies for discussion.

As well as coming to understand how this particular group of artists is using computers to service their researching and art making needs, the investigation also considers how the computer is using these artists through a process of reworking their manual art making procedures and their aesthetic sensibilities. For instance, the Internet, which offers the artists a virtual mobility for information gathering, has also encouraged a dependency on its use founded on efficiency and access. This dependency is in some ways the antithesis to an often perceived overload of information that, as many of the artists remarked, can become an incredible waste of time as they plow through the virtual excess to get to the data they need. In contrast, this new found "virtual mobility" provides the same artist freedom from traditionally constructed constraints of space and time and allows them access to information regardless of it being relevant to their needs (Friedberg 1998:261).

Collins suggests that Internet users and web surfers are becoming much savvier in combating a sensory overload with new "strategies of absorption," bringing information technologies not only to "street level," (1995:16) but also into our living rooms and homes (p.25). These strategies of absorption also call for reconceptualizing our viewing practices. In order to wade through computerized information like the increasing onslaught of visual advertising and stimulus in our day to day environments, artists, like the rest of us are developing an efficiency for dealing with a large quantity of data, finding ways of editing out unwanted information and focusing in on what is needed. New strategies and viewing practices enable the artist to find information more readily through electronic needs, yet, reciprocally building a sense of dependency driven by an ever increasing need for access and effectiveness. Hence, these tools of productivity have the potential to deceptively commandeer the artist into dependency as the function and "cultural resonances" of these technologies fundamentally change our understanding of information technology (p. 16). As Baudrillard suggests, the technological form is testing the human, not the other way around (1983:120).

I believe these issues are central to understanding how artists, as well as many others, are negotiating complex connectivity. Also in this process and through their work, they constitute new meanings that are put forward for the rest of us to interpret in relation to our own negotiations.

**Reconceptualizing manual art making in a digital culture**

For many of us, artists in particular, the Web has developed as a popular public site providing voluminous opportunities for distributing and receiving images and text through a continuous flow of information. This nonstop access is promoting a new digital aesthetic that is influencing the ways in which various individuals from all sectors of society visualize the world. As a result, aesthetics are no longer driven by theory alone, but rather by what currently exists, what is part of the current vision (Gigliotti 2000).

The Web has also presented new burdens to receiving visual representations. The Web adds many levels of stimulus and "the social multiplication of images" (Friedberg 1998:253) that emerge because of the increased reproduction and dissemination of "the visual," challenging the ways, and the rate of speed in which individuals form meaning. Historically, modern individuals (artists included) found ways of shaping themselves to edit out stimuli in the immediate environment in order to give attention to particular details (Buck-Morss 1992; Crary 2000). However, as the myth of individualistic autonomy is further questioned by factors such as globalization and connectivity, reconceptualizing the ways in which all individuals currently view the world becomes increasingly more important with the additional influx of visual stimuli imposed by new media (Crary 2000; Duncum 1999a, 1999b, 2001).

Reconceptualization promotes the development of new strategies of absorption that help prevent individuals, particularly computer users, from becoming bewildered by what might first appear as an overabundance of information. A reconceptualized reading of both current viewing practices and information management opens up the possibilities of access to a world of information through image, text, movement, and sound, that can be attained, archived, manipulated, and reproduced (Collins 1995). Reconceptualized perspectives of computer and digital culture including cyberspace, have the potential to open up new forms of pedagogy that impact on art education. The dialectics and dialogues that develop for artists as they negotiate between physical and virtual worlds, become principal points for learning as they describe the pleasures and the consequences of integrating their grounded, manual ways of making art with their new computer-assisted processes.

It is important to note, however, that this dialectic that I am examining is not necessarily new, or contingent on the postmodern condition. Batchen contends that in the Foucauldian concept of power and subjectivity, the modern subject was always "produced with the interstices of a continual negotiation of real and virtual" (1998:277). Foucault's concept of panopticism offers a model of virtuality where the self is both subjectified and objectified. The self emerges at the threshold of modernity as an "empirico-transcendental doublet" (Foucault 1970:318). Furthermore, these theories have been used to describe a subject that is always divided from itself as a result of exploring a perceivable difference between the real and the virtual, thereby creating a self that is always in relation to a "replicant self, the one floating before us in virtual space" (Batchen 1998:278). The ways in which we understand and experience the real and the virtual are called into question. Moreover, how do we relate this understanding to cyberspace, popularly termed "the virtual" and the increased computerization of everyday routines?

Why is it so important that the current viewing practices of artists be seen as reconceptualized in relation to their ways of working? Perhaps working with computers presents a different form of virtuality from what Batchen contends (via Foucault) has been evident throughout modernity. The form of virtuality I refer to in relation to my investigation of the six artists is characterized by the exchanging and merging of many selves within computerized environments. The artists whose stories are included in this book are in a transitional stage of merging and reconceptualizing the ways they used to view the world and, in turn, they are opening up new possibilities for future ways of working. These are issues that are inherent in their words. Understanding how artists overall are reconceptualizing their viewing and working practices is particularly important in relation to the interstices between their physical and virtual worlds as cyberspace becomes a critical mediator for cultural dialogue.

New interpretations of society evolve as artists also reconceptualize their experiences of the world through a variety of contexts. Closely examining specific artists' experiences of making art in relation to how they develop their manual practices within a digital context requires a thorough unearthing of the kinds of experiences that challenge these artists. Some experiences occur outside the artist. Those are the things (people, places, events etc.) out in the world the artists describe as provoking them to make some form of visual representation. There are experiences inherent in the ways they research their ideas: plotting, developing, and proceeding through a process of trial and error. As well, there are the experiences of physically manipulating materials during handmade art production. Yet, in all these cases, *experience* is already an interpretation of events or interactions. Through visual experimentation, artists continue to investigate, often focusing on the differences in the various contexts and systems within which those experiences occur, contesting or challenging the way things are seen (Scott 1992). Experience is "not the origin of our explanation," but it is that which provides explanations and opens up new ways for considering change (p.38).

More complex experiences are produced when the artists grapple with new digital imaging programs or the Internet in an effort to embrace both their familiar real world and the not so familiar virtual world. These experiences are all ways of becoming. They are played out through the dialectical relationship between the artists' manual self and their digital self. Through reflection and reconceptualization the artist comes to understand this dialectic as their way of being in the world, represented by "the explicit focus of [their] endeavours" (Mulhall 1996:4).

Other contexts that artists experience are the cyber arcades of the Web. These postmodern reconceptions of the nineteenth century windows described by Walter Benjamin (1968) offer new forms of virtual mobility and the opportunity to consume an endless array of imagery. The cyber arcades are dominated by a consumer culture intrigued by new conceptions of speed, novelty, spectacle, and innovation that are computer driven, all of which challenge traditional labour intensive ways of working by hand. They present an electronic shopping mall continuously and excessively stocked with images available for appropriation, reproduction, and dissemination. Within these arcades artists are virtually mobile subjects released from fixed patterns of time and space (Friedberg 1995). They are also virtually released from their fixed location. The artists have access to the image, text and sound banks from a variety of locations within the cyber connections. This combination of access and connectivity can be both disruptive and tantalizing to the artist who is accustomed to working independently in their perceived fixed location of the studio.

The cyber arcades of the Web and the digital manipulation capabilities of computer programs such as Paintbrush have further challenged artists through an ever increasing and incessant production of simulacra. Within the virtual world, the computer becomes the "interlocutor" destined however, in its operations to be "ceaselessly compared" to the artists' more anachronistic ways of working (Baudrillard 1983:93). This particular concern of simulacra is fundamental to the manual/digital dialogue that emerges as the artists continually compare new ways of working digitally with older ways of working manually.

Baudrillard's three phases or orders of simulacra within the postmodern culture provide useful backlighting for examining a particular shift in thinking about the essence of art making in relation to computer-based production and reproduction of imagery. The original handmade work of the artist such as painting or drawing is already a form of first-order simulacra, always revealing detectable differences between the real and the simulated. The machine however, in this case a computer, spawns the second order of simulacra. The second order erases differences and liquefies *the real* within the system of production. With the intervention of the machine, the artist leaves behind what Baudrillard describes as the "counterfeit" object (the handmade work) and enters into reproduction (1983:96). It is through reproduction that the process of the production, the producer, and the product are absorbed into one hegemonic unit (pp. 96-97). On the other hand, the artist may not see themselves as a counterfeiter of the natural real world, but rather someone who autonomously creates impressions of that world. They may not consider their work as simulacra. Some artists may be somewhat disturbed to think of themselves as reproduction specialists or one who continually produces simulacra within a larger system of production. In the capitalist art market, *reproductions* are analogous to fakes and perceived as far less valuable than *originals*. For some artists, the computer is viewed as a tool for reproduction rather than creation. This prompts resistance to new possibilities for making art and images.

The issue of reproducing simulacra may cause a disconcerting situation for the artist who considers the making of reproductions to be contrary to their grounded sense of themselves as hand-makers of original works of art. This shift between first order and second order simulacra was also described by Benjamin (1968) as a loss of the aura. The loss occurs as the work of art is released from fixed spatial and temporal positions by means of its reproduction thereby challenging the role of the static original (Benjamin 1968:220). This dispossession is reconstituted by many artists who view computerization as a threat to the hand workings of their profession. Losing the aura of the original is interpreted as a loss of society's need for handmade art production. Many artists see the rise of simulacra as the disintegration in value of the art object which affects their standard way of life. This particular point of view prompts cynicism and resistance toward forms of image production that are computer-based and therefore infinitely reproduce able on a much greater scale than what has been accomplished before.

Collins argues that through information technologies and cyberspace, the aura is not lost, but rather it has "proliferated" through a multiplication and dispersal of information that has, for the most part, a great deal of personal investment from a diversity of authors both known and unknown (1995:25). Collins' theory complements Baudrillard's third order of simulacra. This level of simulacra production has particular implications for artists who are integrating computer technology with their manual image and text production processes. The third order of simulacra is *serial production* where works are "conceived from the point-of-view of their very reproducibility" (Baudrillard 1983:100). It is within this third order of simulacra that everything proceeds from a model instead of an original. At this level images may be appropriated from the Web or conceived on a computer screen. Accordingly, these images may be manipulated, reproduced and distributed without a hard copy original. The six artists interviewed for the study have begun to explore the third level of simulacra, some more hesitantly than others. They are discovering new ways of developing ideas and questioning their existing assumptions of "the original work of art."

As a result of the many shifts in perception about "real" and "virtual" worlds and the effect of simulacra, artists are confronted by a hyper-phantasmagoria (a new kind of accelerated seduction of the power of illusion) that induces a new and sometimes uncontested politics of aesthetics that drives visual literacies and forms of meaning making (Gigliotti 2000; Keifer-Boyd 1996; Mercedes 1996). The handmade work of these artists is continuously challenged by the inherent seduction of digital imaging and manipulation. Artists' stories about their experiences of creating in physical and virtual worlds provide insightful data for analyzing the consequences of *being digital* across a variety of contexts. Furthermore, the storied accounts illustrate the ways in which older modes of working are refracted emerging as changed in some way and never quite the same after translation, thus prompting the artists to reconsider their practices.

**Contextualizing the artists' new ways of working and making**

The artists' stories illuminate some of the influencing variables that are affecting their idea development and bring to light the impact of new technologies such as the Internet and the Web on those developments. A new form of dialogue occurs when the artists begin to reconceptualize their viewing practices and reconstruct familiar ways of making within not-so-familiar contexts. Computers and the Internet provide new portals or windows for these artists to see distant places and people. As well, the incessant access to information on the Web presents an abundance of stimuli that is vying for the artists' attention. These are new challenges to receiving visual representations, adding multiple levels of imagery that problematize the ways and contexts in which meaning can be formed.

Like the rest of us using computers and surfing the abundant resources on the Web, artists are quickly becoming information managers as they learn to sift through pages of data in the process of creating meaning on multiple levels through various contexts. New cyber-cultures and visual languages that have been created also present networks of diverse communities which challenge and influence traditional artists' concept of the self and creative practice. The early work of Turkle (1995) and Rheingold (1993) on the emergence of virtual communities suggests that a great number of individuals including many artists (in the first world) are now interconnected, living in both physical and virtual worlds. It appears that "being digital" has come into a praxis for those individuals who comfortably wield the computer mouse, digitizing their cultural production and engaging with others in cyberspace (Negroponte 1995). For many, computers have become embedded into daily routines, school work and household management, yet they are less transparent in other aspects of work. For several artists the act of moving between manual processes and digital ways of working and being in the studio has not yet reached a comfort zone. As a former painter now negotiating a computerized world, I feel this lack of comfort felt by numerous artists has not been closely examined or articulated.

For the most part, the work of artists often reflects the cultural shifts occurring in society at large. Artists' work questions the effects of various emergent contexts and environments on individuals, including themselves (De Kerckhove 1995). Historically, research has addressed trends in artists' uses of digital technology to create imagery (Dinkla 1996; Gigliotti 2000; Goodman 1987; Helfand 2001; Hershman Leeson 1996; Huhtamo 1996; Paterson 1999), but to date has not examined the influence of digital or computer culture and the Web on the handmade production of images through art making.

Much of the current discourse tends to centre on artists' problematizing and conceptualizing the interface between humans and machines as the subject matter of their work. Some early studies examine the introduction of artificial intelligence systems that simulated art making (Cohen 1988; Morbey 1993, 1994, 1995). This does not emphasize the effects of computers on the artists themselves by providing a focus on the ways in which they have altered, or not, how they develop and produce art images despite the chosen subject matter. Alternatively, I have chosen to examine the dichotomies and dialogues between handmade and digital processes artists employ, that is the relation of integration and exchange between these modalities in their exploration of ideas and production of imagery in the process of art making.

Three particular contexts have been used to explore the relationships and interchanges between manual and digital procedures the artists are experimenting with to create imagery. These include autobiographical contexts, social contexts and technological contexts. All of these contexts can be investigated individually, and then again as overlapping locations where each artist works from time to time. As artists do not work in a vacuum, isolated from external or internal variables, these contexts are important for understanding how the artists' stories shift from one location of self to another.

The experiences that present themselves to the artists as autobiographical are interpreted and reconceptualized as texts that relate to each other across their stories and reinterpreted in the study findings presented in chapters 3 and 4. Grumet (1981) describes reconceptualization as the "means to conceive again, to turn back the conceptual structures that support our actions in order to reveal the rich and abundant experience they conceal" (p.139). Yet, through these actions, we are not just conceiving again, rather we have the opportunity to constitute new meaning through our own forms of intertextuality. Intertextuality in this sense, Barthes (1977) writes, considers the artist as author of her life where her life "is no longer the origin of [her] fictions but a fiction contributing to [her] work; there is a reversion of the work onto the life" (p.161).

Furthermore, the artists' experiences are reconceptualized through my reinterpretations and re-workings of their texts into my texts. The reconceptualized texts explore and examine questions of computer use that derive from my own art practice and are reconstituted later on in chapter 7 on a macro level through a discussion of implications that affect the broader art community. There is a reversion of these macro level texts back onto the artists who participate within larger art worlds.

The artists' experiences within social contexts are conceived as the public face of art making production where the artist is drawn into communicating with others and participating in the larger art world community. The work of the artist is often perceived as an isolated practice, executed within the confines of a solitary studio. However, this is not the case. Artists are affected by the discourses of economics, politics, other social groups and cultural workers. Art is produced in a collective/social environment, as a form of social production, "in a mutual relation of interdependence with social structures," and affected by the larger system of capitalist enterprise (Wolff 1993:9). The introduction of computers into the working procedures of artists includes socially constructed assumptions and perceptions regarding the computerization of everyday life and work. Potentially these assumptions affect the artists' own perceptions toward the mechanization and computerization of processes that have traditionally been viewed as handmade. The labour intensity of these procedures has often been relational to market value and the working status of the artist.

Social commentary regarding the encroachment of computers into daily living and working routines can be either encouraging or detrimental depending on the level of technological determinism. Becker (2002) describes artists as "caught in the discourse of the times, adding to these discourses with imagery and language, and then judged by how well their innovations bring clarity to the historical moment" (p.23). The artists are judged not only by others in the broader art community and society at large, but they also self-judge their own actions in the process of creating new meaning about the world as they strive to establish new comfort levels with technology and understand where they fit in. All of these factors within the social context that contribute to the narrative, or fiction as Barthes calls it, of the artists' lives become part of their work. Reciprocally, their work is their life. Art making, whether it is manually produced or digitally realized, is cultural production that takes place within the capitalist market-culture that we all participate in.

Another context for examining the artists' experiences is the realm of technology. For Heidegger, on one level the technological represents the "manufacture and utilization of equipment, tools, and machines, the manufactured and used things themselves" that the artists employ for making art (1977:4). In the case of my research this involves procedures that are both handmade and computer driven, some of which may provoke a "push-pull" relationship between processes based within both physical and virtual worlds. However for Heidegger, the realm of technology is not merely limited to instrumentally defined procedures of manufacturing. Rather, technologies are ways of "bringing forth" and revealing, enabling artists to "bring something into appearance" (p. 9). The artists, like their materials, are not solely responsible for the thing that is made as the thing is imbued with other forms of techne that constitute its being (pp.7-9). While Heidegger states "[i]nstrumentality is considered to be the fundamental characteristic of technology . . . Technology is a way of revealing" (p.12). This bringing forth or "poiēsis", is key not only for looking at the way the artists develop their practices across multiple contexts, but also for understanding the artists' own ways of becoming, literally of becoming someone different (p.34). The realm of technology in this sense is a way of both bringing forth something new and of self-making through autopoiēsis.

While each of these three different contexts may be examined in isolation, they are inextricably linked. These three particular contexts back-light the study artists' dialogue with broader social and cultural issues. Backlighting the conversations promote a broader investigation by opening up questions around how the artists are negotiating through both physical and virtual or digital worlds, underlining the points at which they are most comfortable with their various working processes and at which points they are most challenged. Furthermore, backlighting the conversations explores the different conditions and situations that prompt artists to exchange and integrate digital and manual procedures from more than one perspective. Attention to multiple perspectives helps to highlight particular moments when the artists are stimulated, excited, apprehensive, or resistant when they immerse themselves in their work.

### Conceptualizing the artists' stories as phenomenologically-based data

I have chosen to initiate my examination of the artists' stories using a phenomenological perspective as a way of gaining access to the experiences embedded in integrating manual and digital processes as a way of making art and becoming an artist. The conversations between me and the artists are collectively intertwined with the cultural phenomena surrounding the physical and virtual world contexts I have been describing. Those contexts affect the ways in which we construct ourselves as artists and how we reinterpret our experiences under different conditions. Conversations with the artists suggest that their different approaches to art making are related to their location of self within both physical and virtual worlds. Recognizing these relationships opens up the possibility of a variety of learning experiences that can guide the artists toward a mutable sense of self within a world of complex connectivity.

In light of my focus on the contextual backlighting of the artists' stories, my choice of beginning with a phenomenological perspective is due to the complementarity of art making and phenomenology. Both strive to convey multiple aspects of an experience. The multiple aspects exist as both inside and outside influences that are autobiographical, social, political and economical. Phenomenology requires a continuous return to the experience of the lived world, asking the question "what is it like to have a certain experience?" (Van Manen 1982: 296). The phenomenologically studied experience requires a responsive critical reading where the reader is asked to pay attention to what is said and what is not said. It is a way of making visible and apparent, that which is usually hidden. Making visible those elements of life that may be perceived as hidden is also the job of artists.

An extensive investigation of the impact of computers on fine art production is called for. I have engaged in a critical analysis of the artists' stories as an attempt to excavate the broader implications regarding computer/human interface research that are inherent in their experiences and their descriptive dialogue. A critical reading of the artists' experiences therefore also calls for a deconstructive approach to analyzing the conversations that, in Derridian fashion, disrupts, rearranges, and then reconstructs those experiences. My objective here is to deconstruct the complexities of the artists' experiences by using the repetitions and the contradictions embedded in their dialogue and the language they use. The resulting work is a re-thinking of art-making practice as a mutable form of cultural production that involves multiple selves dispersed across both physical and virtual worlds.

The importance of this research lies in the possibility of reconceptualizing traditional art-making practices within the context of a digital culture. Moreover, emerging theories regarding the developing dialectic between the manual and digital artist-selves opens up the possibility of a hybrid form of maker. Questions about the integration or exchange of manual and digital processes in relation to art making practice have not been considered. For many of the artists, the conversations both answered existing questions that they had not been able to articulate before, as well as provoking new questions about their processes which provide a clearer understanding of the challenges and the bonuses of integrating computer technology into Fine Art practice. Furthermore, this research also contributes to the sparse literature that exists on art making practice, particularly within a Canadian context. More specifically, material concerning artists' interfaces with computers during the various stages of an art making practice that primarily relies on manual procedures such as painting is almost nonexistent.

Particular aspects of the artists' dialogue illuminate their self-conscious perceptions of the behaviours inherent in the exploratory and creative engagements that take place in between and across physical and virtual working environments. While my particular research focuses on visual artists' working environments, there is also the possibility that behaviours demonstrated by an individual's resistance to technology and their eventual seduction by that technology as seen through the study participants' stories, may extend to other contexts, raising questions regarding our awareness of how we engage technology.

## The scope of the case study research

One of the overriding assumptions inherent in the case studies I present is that all the artists I interviewed are to a great extent cognizant of their own working processes and recognize how they select and prepare ideas for presentation as works of art. I am also presuming that the artists identify themselves as *artists*, and thus in some way, identify with others in the broader art community. The artists' stories provide the foundational data on which I base my new theories which are analyzed more extensively in chapters 5 and 6.

I also see the case study research as being affected by two particular variables. Firstly, by the criteria I used to select the six artists and secondly by my own definitions of *artist* and *art making* practices. The six artists who were interviewed for the micro case studies only work in traditional two-dimensional media such as painting or drawing. My participant selection criteria exclude those who work primarily in sculpture, installation, time-based and computer-based art. I consider painting and drawing as *mark-making* activities leading to the production of images within a two-dimensional frame (paper or canvas) or screen. I see a workable comparison of these handmade images to those digitally produced for the computer screen which also presents images within a frame. Three-dimensional sculptures, time-based and computer-based art complicates a direct comparison of handmade production using formal properties such as line, colour and form with digital manipulation that considers the same properties in similar, yet different ways. The mark making works are presented on single screen formats, whereas digital work on the Internet can be presented through multiple windows and screens and for this reason, may already be considered time-based. The essence of my comparison and analysis lies in the interchanges between analog and digital procedures for producing what are two dimensional representations, although many new media artists may not consider screen representations as strictly two dimensional. All the artists participating in this study are web savvy and consistently turn to information on the Web when investigating a query they may have, regardless of subject matter or use.

The second variable that influences how this study is positioned is my own definition regarding artists and their practices. This definition of art making and art practice has been constructed in part by my own experiences as a practicing visual artist and may appear exclusive to others in the larger art community. In such work I define art making practice as the representation of ideas and concepts using images which, on occasion, incorporate text. This activity is a regular practice and part of the artist's life work. I make the assumption that artists produce tangible objects as a result of exploring their ideas. My definition is by no means inclusive, but it represents my own perceptions of artists and art making and underscores who I invited to participate in the study.

The data used to explore the research question is limited to the connections between how this particular group of artists explores ideas when making art, the navigational strategies they use when investigating a subject or idea on the Web, their experiences with digital and image manipulating computer programs and how they articulate their experiences. The results are specific to the manual/digital dialectics that develop for these artists. The results of this study should be viewed as exploratory and not generalizable to all artists regardless of medium, working processes or technical experiences. This study is part of a grander project in process as all of us experiment with the integration of new technologies within our daily living and working routines. The experiences of the six artists however, propose new perspectives and possibilities surrounding manual and digital collaborative experiences offering other artists and art educators a position from which they may question their own current practices.

# CHAPTER TWO: RETHINKING ART MAKING PRACTICES

This chapter presents a set of conceptual lenses to be used for viewing the six artists' stories which are an integral part of my research. I am suggesting that the artists' accounts be considered in these very particular ways. The lenses have been developed using current literature across varied discourses, including those concerned with art education. My objective for this chapter is to put forward different perspectives on art making that are to be considered while contemplating the artists' accounts (threaded throughout chapters three and four) of their experiences of integrating computers into their manual practices of producing images and making art. My purpose is twofold. First, the lenses I offer derive from particular Western-modernist perceptions about art making. This helps to see the six artists' stories as located within a context that is often historically situated in Western terms. While this perspective is obviously exclusive, it does provide an understanding of the particular historical context in which the artists have developed their practices.

Secondly, by highlighting these different perspectives as conceptual lenses I am afforded the opportunity to see what is missing, found in the gaps and deficiencies in the literature that currently exists. Examining these gaps and deficiencies is important to understanding what work still needs to be done. This includes recognizing new directions that can be explored through dialoguing with artists who are striving and struggling to integrate both physical and virtual ways of making into their image production.

These conceptual lenses are not being presented because they provide an absolute and all-inclusive perspective of the way things are in artistic practice.

Rather, as Dienst (1995:x) suggests, I see them as an "invention of theoretical images" that link up with the images produced by the artists' own words which, in turn, are used here in the service of developing new theories. The five particular lenses I am presenting offer perspectives on:

i) the artists work as a form of meaning making about the world,

ii) reconsidering the places and spaces where artists make work,

iii) rethinking the image production of artists as a form of visual culture,

iv) making connections between old and new ways of making art,

v) overcoming scepticism by developing new languages for making art and images.

**Studying artists making art and making meaning**

Through their work, artists produce images as a way of connecting with and making meaning from their experiences (Jongeward 1997). Their production of many works over time reinterprets those experiences, revisiting them through different contexts. While artists may be perceived as self-constructing individuals on the one hand (Watrin 1999), they cannot escape the social structures and spaces in which they live and work, or the contestable, historical situatedness of their profession. Although they may appear to make work autonomously, they tend to produce knowledge within a system of shared meanings and social interaction, that being our culture (Blumer, 1969). Artists do not merely reflect the world as it is, but rather, reinterpret what they see in relation to their own notions of culture "by constructing models of reality" that inform their actions and help them bring meaning to how they experience the world (James 1996:147). They reconstitute meaning rather than reflect what is already apparent.

In this way, artists become a kind of conduit through which meaning is rerouted, and reconsidered. When placed on display outside the studio environment, the artists' work becomes publicly pedagogical. The work offers possibilities for opening up new ways to view and experience the world from other perspectives, however mindful that those experiences are already an interpretation of particular encounters. Artists' interpretations can thus be perceived as mutable, "contestable," and changeable over time (Scott 1992:35).

Artists, me included, pose questions about their connection to the world and how that relationship is ever-changing and in flux. Posing questions through image production is a way that artists attempt to investigate different aspects of themselves and others around them. In this way, they can better see their position in the world and their relationship to others. Becker maintains that these "essential goals" have not changed even though society and the technological environment that artists now work within have undergone tremendous change (2002:27). How artists achieve these goals however, has become more complex with the introduction and ensuing integration of digital manipulation programs and emergent communications technologies that offer new ways of producing imagery.

Some artists such as Antoinette Herival (1997) have gone so far as to self-examine their own art making procedures in an effort to understand their processes of working and meaning making. Herival studied her own art practice for a five-month period through a reflective diary and technical working notes. She maintains that "relating to everyday incidents enabled me to see a larger pattern of behaviour which connected to the way in which I found knowledge through art making" (p.56). Herival's experiment provided her with a multidimensional perspective of how and why she was constructing meaning through her work.

Not all artists however, are interested in researching their own behaviours. Most are involved in understanding how they conceptually interpret the world around them and how they technically manifest those interpretations through images and objects. Many do not engage in examining their own behaviours, exploring how they think about making, why they choose particular directions over others, or how their routines are affected by change and new technological innovation within their working environments. Yet, these are important questions to ask in light of new demands that are bestowed on those artists who are working in both physical and virtual contexts, integrating digital processes with traditional, manual procedures.

The process of art making in any context involves the production of meaning through symbolic structures and acts affected by the artists' interpretations of experience, and their consumption of currently existing cultural and historical metanarratives (Blandy & Congdon 1987; Felshin 1995; Gablik 1991; Phillips 1995). In this way, art making practice is perceived as socially constructed and filtered through the socialization of the artist (Wolff, 1993). Artist practitioners are consumers of cultural influences and norms and their processes and products are representations of cultural consumption that is communicated visually (sometimes aurally), and often challenged by changes in mainstream technologies. However, meaning that is constituted within the messages communicated by artists, is not always straightforward because what artists produce "registers the messy vitality of the world" in nonlinear ways that often break with conventional patterns of meaning making (Phillips 1995:170).

The consequences of these nonlinear ways of working affect the artists' process of researching, thinking and making. Artists move through "a labyrinth of commodified light and noise, endeavouring to piece together bits of dispersed narrative" (Kearney 1988:13), sometimes emphasizing the disjointed peculiarities that develop. The artists become postmodern bricoleurs of a multitude of diverse fragments that are culled from a conglomerate of socially produced experiences and interactions. The task of mixing-up, collaging and juxtaposing images in order to create new meaning within physical contexts becomes more complex in virtual worlds because of further fragmentation.

Traditionally, artists' ways of making meaning concentrated on the making of art objects through the study of form, composition, colour theory, and the conceptual development of ideas through content. In postmodern culture however, meaning-making that is rooted in art making has shifted from concerns about the aesthetic object toward issues of power. Clark contends that in relation to art making "meaning is seen as a socially constructed entity, requiring the viewer to look beyond the formalist compositional qualities of a work, decode its symbolic imagery, and expose its embedded cultural assumptions" (1996:2). What happens however, when the familiar modes of making art are disrupted? As artists continue to produce images in physical and now virtual contexts, the decoding becomes more complex, cultural assumptions become multiplicitous, thereby expecting the viewers' interpretations to also become mobile and mutable across various spatial and temporal locations. Interpretations become socially, culturally and politically interchangeable as the production of meaning is no longer confined to a static fixed object. The materiality and value of the art object are contested as it moves between physical and virtual worlds. This opens up questions about how the effects of interchanging the two modalities within the artist's studio affect the ways in which meaning is reinterpreted, and then later reconstituted at the level of the viewer. The ways in which meaning-making changes for different artists, depending on context or modality (physical or virtual) is one particular lens for looking at the artists' stories that contribute to this research.

## Rethinking the studio: Other places and spaces for making art

The physical site for art making known quite commonly as the studio, has historically been a space that Lash suggests is "lifted out from routine forms of life" (2001:114). More recently he contends it has become a laboratory for creating prototypes and products that reinterpret cultural activity and suggest new meanings in the everyday. Lash's rethinking of the studio space brings into focus two particular important issues. The first is the cultural assumption surrounding the location of where artists work, and secondly, the forms of production that are undertaken in these particular locations. Rethinking the studio as a laboratory opens up the possibilities for artists to become, not so much creators of art objects, but researchers attending to issues of cultural and pedagogical significance. The laboratory context is mutable in that it can shift between physical and virtual modalities depending on the direction of the research and the form of visual representation chosen by the artist. The autonomous painter working at the easel with pungent smelling oil paint is one of the romantic images being contested here.

The laboratory becomes a place where digital prototypes may be exchanged or integrated with manual procedures as the project moves forward. Artists explore and research their ideas and develop prototypes that demonstrate one process or medium integrated with another. In the laboratory, the artist has the opportunity to reconsider fixed conceptions of the studio space, the place of the art object, and changing representations of the world based on new interrelations. They have opportunities to experiment and develop multiple forms of representation through prototypes of production processes and image development, proposing new possibilities of the way things could be.

Castells defines place as "a locale whose form, function and meaning are self-contained within the boundaries of physical contiguity" (1996:423). This could describe many modernist perceptions of what the artist's studio is . . . an actual fixed place of work. However, these places or studios are not really fixed in another sense, but are the result of intersecting social relations and processes (Probyn 1990, Massey 1994). Harvey asks "by what social process(es) is place constructed?" (1993:5). What are the social processes and assumptions that construct the "real" place of the artist's studio as well as the virtual spaces they are inventing within their computers, also a place where they work? While Castells opts for a new spatial logic he terms "space of flows" (1996: 378) that better accommodates questions of space and place within the new informational economy, Harvey contends that "place-bound identities" remain important as new spatial organizations including the Internet and the Web develop (1993:4).

Issues of place and space are increasingly important to artists as they consider their home computer as another type of place for making art. The computer offers a virtual space within the physical confinement of the fixed place of the studio. While the territorial-based studio is a place to go to for making art, the computer within that locale extends the opportunity to develop "practices that invent spaces" in virtual worlds (De Certeau, 1999:133). The ways in which the places and spaces where artists make art and produce images are socially constructed, affect how they negotiate these terrains in both physical and virtual worlds. This becomes complicated if the artists retain a "territorial place-based identity" (Harvey 1993:4). Is who they are as artists tied to the places and spaces where they make work? Rethinking the studio as a laboratory place and /or a virtual space outside the artists' usual fixed locale for working, offers another lens through which to view the actions and articulations of artists at work.

**Rethinking art and image making as forms of visual culture**

Art making practices including the area of art education and the visual arts have emerged as forms of cultural production that often traverse traditionally constructed boundaries (Freedman 2000:316; see also Duncum 1997). This is evident in the diversity of images that are used in advertising, the aesthetic sensibilities appropriated from advertising forms and incorporated within contemporary painting, the interweaving of film, video and new media into art installations and the blurring of the borders between anything digital. This is due in part to a conceptual shift facilitated by postmodernism where artists are "revisit[ing] social content and reveal[ing] historical connections to their art and popular culture" (Freedman 2000:320). The act of revisiting and deconstructing the borders between "art" and "culture" has also prompted artists to ask questions and challenge established metanarratives and segregated disciplines, many of which stem from a Eurocentric partitioning of the High or Fine arts from everyday experiences. Artists are emphasizing the social dimensions of art rather than just art's formal and technical characteristics such as line, form, colour, and composition. The emerging bricolage created when artists appropriate and include popular, or social/political images into their cultural production has challenged the "purist" disciplines established in High art schools such as modernist painting. The shift away from the perception of making art as a form of total invention toward the "re-articulation" of existing cultural codes (Collins 1995: 92) has broadened the discipline of visual arts, merging it with the emerging and all-inclusive field of study called visual culture.

Visual Culture has become a wide-ranging domain for exploring the continuing development of the visual arts, visual representations, and art making practices in an environment where cultures and contexts collide. This current shift toward visual culture is important to current visual arts research because it opens up art making to a multitude of contexts and locations that include cyberspace and digital image production. The Web is one example of a vehicle that is related to both popular culture and visual culture. It is increasingly used as a tool for research, image appropriation and dissemination by many artists. Important concepts to note, particularly in relation to the theories I develop throughout my research, are the ways in which the six artists interviewed dissolve traditional disciplinary boundaries within their modes of cultural production and see the opportunities to work across different media distinctions both technically through art making, and conceptually in relation to how they think about themselves as image producers, not just painters or artists who draw.

Art making practice and cyber culture are sited within a number of discourses that use multiple theories to interpret the interactions and exchanges offered by each. However, it is the field of study labeled "visual culture" that we can use to explore the intertextuality of all things visual in everyday life. Visual culture recognizes that a broad range of visual forms is "concerned with visual events in which information, meaning, or pleasure is sought by the consumer in an interface with visual technology" (Mirzoeff 1999:3). This shift challenges static examinations of the art object within traditional institutions, and instead, proposes an inclusive study of all that is visible, and "represents a recognition of a vastly changed cultural environment, which includes a new symbiosis between new technologies, new economic arrangements, and changed social formations" (Duncum 2001:103).

The arena of visual culture defies traditional compartmentalizing of all things visual into high and low forms of cultural representations such as the academic classifications and systems traditionally used to identify the Fine arts (Elkins 2001:50). Elkins contends that there are only a few "ideal methods" of producing imagery as all others are dependent on the very few languages that exist to think about media. He says that "artists can be seduced into thinking that each medium is independent of its predecessors, when it may take decades for that to happen" (p.52). Furthermore, Elkins maintains that artists often focus on what is truly unique (or apparently innovative) about a chosen medium, forfeiting the ideal methods that have historically been the foundation of that media through its application (e.g. painting) and surrounding discourse. To this end he describes computer graphics as pixilated images whose ideal methods are still grounded in re-presenting nineteenth and twentieth century modernist painting (Elkins 2001:54).

The field of visual culture however, eschews traditional thinking about creating visual representations by undermining the master narratives that are the foundations of modernist formalizations and underpin those "ideal methods." If we are to agree with Elkins and understand visual representations as largely all deriving from a few ideal methods (i.e., the formal considerations of presenting ideas through colour, composition, form and symbol) we must understand these methods as mutable across various media forms, in both physical and virtual contexts.

Although I maintain that Elkins' theory is contestable, he does offer another important lens for considering the six study artists' accounts of their methods and procedures for making art. All of the artists interviewed make their art from a grounded position that is dependent on the ideal methods that Elkins attaches to modernist painting. The artists are indeed working toward unfixing their static approaches to these methods by transferring their working procedures to virtual contexts. However, they all still describe their ways of working and the characteristics of the images produced using many of the same properties in Elkins' report.

Traditionally, the visual arts through institutionalized modernism have been perceived as High culture, a position that transcends the popular production of culture through everyday interaction. In this way, Trend contends that there is a standing perception that "great art' is construed as an array of objects that exist beyond the lives and productive capabilities of ordinary people" (1992:5). High culture often proliferate Eurocentric master narratives which portray the work of artists as building on past visions and representations. These portrayals are frequently dismissive of current social and cultural contexts. Through these master narratives, popular culture is disdained and resisted because of its "addiction to novelty" which dismisses traditionally constructed aesthetics and value systems (Varnedoe & Gopnik 1990). New approaches to visual representations through a carnivalesque use of popular culture, however, dislodges the Eurocentric foundations of aesthetics (on which Elkins ideal methods were founded) and turn them upside down in favour of locating a new kind of popular beauty (Shohat & Stam 1998). The carnivalesque rejects "the construction of an ideal language of beauty in relation to which other types are seen as inferior, dialectical variations" (p.36).

New media, digital manipulation programs and certainly the Web, all invite different forms of the carnivalesque into the production of imagery. The carnivalesque has a seductive power that has many artists exchanging modernist versions of beauty for simulated forms that have the capability through computer driven programs and systems, to mutate and reproduce in ways that Baudrillard's (1983) third order of simulacra has already professed. In this case, the art objects and images are conceived because of their serial production qualities that easily facilitate reproduction and distribution. Reproduction challenges the romantic notion of the original masterpiece of beauty, a notion often tied to monetary value within a capitalist system of production. These are all issues that challenge the artists' traditional perceptions of what art making is all about.

Looking at how the six study artists produce images not only within the disciplinary boundaries of drawing and painting, but as forms of production that contribute to visual culture, encourages new and diverse interpretations of their ways of making art and making meaning. Their experiences of integrating computers into their production have begun to contest fixed categories of representation, especially divisions of high and low culture. Such categories in the past have denied "the very real ways that we all both consume and produce culture" (Trend 1998:5).

Visual culture then provides the theoretical formulation for exploring the ways in which artists are integrating mainstream digital imaging programs, such as Photoshop, with their traditional manual ways of making art. It also provides the location where the Web can be seen as a mutable vehicle of popular culture, global information access and image distribution centre. The field of visual culture promotes perspectives that open up opportunities for developing new dialogues that redefine how artists, and the rest of us, see the visual patterns of our everyday interactions and experiences.

**Developing connections between older and newer modalities for making art**

Art is "always about something" and demands some sort of interpretation through processes of deconstruction and recoding because it is an expression of another person or group of people (Barrett 1994:71). However, in order to develop an understanding of the "aboutness" of art and how it evolves, the artist's ways of making must "be associated with a critical reading of reality" and recognition that the world may be "reinvented" by imagining it as something other than it currently is (Friere, 1991:24). Art and its making are mutable representations of ever-changing contexts and perceptions that exchange and integrate old ways of working with new.

Art making is a way for particular individuals to be part of the social fabric by marking their experiences through producing visual representations that say: *this is the way I currently see the world around me.* In such rapidly changing times, Dissanayake (cited in Gablik 1995) contends that artists are finding new ways of re-making their experiences by rethinking the connections between past and present encounters (p.44).

Through their participation, the six study artists I interviewed were asked to interrogate the connections they were making between their experiences and interactions with the world and their ways of producing images. They questioned why they took particular approaches and began to find new connections when describing how they used their home computers on a daily basis both in and out of the studio. They opened up questions regarding manual and digital ways of developing and producing images and began to rethink how they could disseminate those images both traditionally through gallery contexts and then again in cyberspace.

Recognizing the ways in which connections are developed between older and newer ways of working helps to provide a foundation for further exploration. The artists can use their knowledge about these connections to move more easily across physical and virtual contexts when making art. As a communicative form of technology however, the visual arts inform and are informed by other media structures. New forms of production are rarely "adopted" Fidler (1997) suggests, without the individual's attempts to make familiar links to earlier existing forms (p.15). This appears as a process where the artists' representations are continually being rethought, remade, their meaning reconstituted, and then presented once again over a period of time. The process may appear cyclical, but instead, it is discontinuous, and the re-making often nonlinear. Furthermore, before the artist works to re-make meaning through new forms of production, they may experience disruptions to their established ways of making art because of questions that arise out of the changing cultural environment. In the case of the artists introduced in chapter 3, these questions are coming from emergent technological changes to many different forms of production.

Moreover, the unmaking of established practices tends to disrupt existing social and cultural assumptions, rousing a disconnection of the artist from familiar and comfortable ground. The artists are further challenged by possible changes to their value systems such as what *things* constitute art in the commercial market, on a conceptual level (Becker 1996; Gablik 1995), by changes to their understanding of the social norms that relate to their art making in terms of reproduction and dissemination procedures (May 1994), by the introduction of new media (Hicks 1993), or by a shift that demands the development of new literacies and/or vocabularies (Duncum 1997; Gigliotti 2000; Logan 2000).

These challenges, shifts, and changes can generate what Fidler calls "mediamorphosis." Historically, our modern and postmodern cultures have been subjected to disruptions brought about by the development of new technologies over and over again. In most cases, we seem susceptible to "surprise" and the belief that our culture is proceeding too rapidly (Fidler 1997:10). Yet, when this happens, according to Fidler's concept of "mediamorphosis," we look for familiar bridges that link what we see as new and innovative with existing and/or earlier media forms and modes of production (p.273). Similarly, art making follows a similar process of recognizing links and then building bridges in order to negotiate procedures for integrating new innovations and untried media into established practices. This, in turn, facilitates a remaking of the art practice with which the artist establishes a comfort zone until there are new disruptions that lead to its unmaking again.

"Mediamorphosis" presents yet another theoretical perspective for exploring how artists can develop connections that afford both handmade and digital technologies for producing images. Recognizable reference points that illuminate common links between drawing by hand and drawing by computer demonstrate how one media form may be embedded within another. This process helps artists develop new relationships across different media forms as they remake and redefine their practices, in both physical and virtual contexts.

### Making way for new forms of image production while regarding past histories

Over time, artists and the contexts for their practices have been affected by a multitude of social, cultural and technological changes. For example, the introduction of photography and later cinematic film broadened the function of the rectangular window created by modernist painting (Manovich 2001). The new windows of photography facilitated the repositioning of subjects, objects and the role of the observer. Modern terms of vision and the introduction of photography defined individuals as both subjects who were also spectators engaged in "the spectacular consumption of images" as well as "observed-observers" who were the subjects of a new age of surveillance (Lalvani, 1996:171). While the use of linear perspective in painting situated the individual as part of a hierarchical order in nature through the gaze of the painter (p.172), the camera obscura, separated the individual from nature. The camera obscura created distinctions between images and objects, and placed the individual as an observer of the world (Crary 1999). Modern twentieth century viewing through photography and cinema initiated the separation and distinguishing between objects and their representations which mediated the viewing of images through apparatuses that were distinct from the artist and the viewer.

Following the technological lineage of photography and film, television also has had a great influence on the art making practice of many artists, particularly those working in the post abstract expressionist and pop art periods. Robert Rauchenberg and Andy Warhol invited the affective influences of television into their practices by constantly working with a television set turned on in their studios. This enabled them to be continuously affected by what was happening in the world outside (Farmer 2000:21). Mediating their practices through the continuous flow of an imaging technology was a strategy both artists used to connect their image production with everyday life on a number of levels. This flow of images and sound has been amplified more recently with the Internet and the Web, both of which have entered many artists' studios giving them what they perceive to be global access to images and information.

Historically however, the influence of technology often sparked pessimistic predictions in regards to the demise of older media with the burgeoning of the new. Lovejoy (1997) draws a parallel between concerns about the effects of electronic technology on art making practices with the concerns and paranoia raised when photography emerged. In 1839, a cultural critic declared that "painting is dead" because of photography (p.23). Furthermore, the introduction of photography was connected to the evolution of the "Machine Age" that prompted the "alienating loss of human connectedness" (p.24). This shift was perceived as the inevitable loss of a human-ness that was grounded in feeling and emotion. Over time however, artists have used photography as both a tool for understanding, creating, and reproducing reality through image production, and also as a medium for expression. Painting has survived and is continuously being reinvented and "mediamorphosized" in response to new cultural and technological conditions.

Yet, the skeptical cries have surfaced again with the insurgence of electronic media and its penetration into the art world and artists' studios. In light of any scepticism, Lovejoy (1997) proclaims that "digital simulation has finally shattered the paradigm of representation we have been operating under since the Renaissance" (p.3). She maintains that artists have new opportunities for working both individually and collaboratively on works that extend beyond the object as those works become interwoven with various communications technologies such as the Internet. This presents a potential shift in how artists perceive art works as having a physical and/or non-physical existence and reveals more fully the myth of *presence* in relation to the function of signifiers in social life.

Throughout modernism and much of postmodernism, art making has primarily been realized via the production of art objects and representations presented in a physical state. The truth in art existed because of these objects and their being. However, as Nietzsche suggests, truth is "a sum of human relations which become poetically and rhetorically intensified, metamorphosed, adorned, and after long usage seem to a notion fixed, canonic, and binding; truths are illusions of which one has forgotten that they are illusions" (1998: 359). As Nietzsche contends, we feel obligated to hold fast to these fixed bonds that have endured time. Yet, when the physicality of the art object is absent, the illusion of representations is put into question and the truth that hinges on the physical presence of canvas, paint, or paper is revealed as an illusion.

Art making is more than just the production of physical objects. It has become part of an ongoing social process that connects individuals through various cultural forms that include signifying and encoding practices. These are not necessarily tied to universal truths about being, value or commodity. This certainly does not trigger the end (again) to older forms of creating and presenting physical art objects, but rather challenges the role of representation in art making and artists' signifying practices, opening up new modes of image production and dissemination. Representation, Lovejoy suggests, is affected by the current cultural vision and by "the nature of the tools" that artists use to create (1997:246).

Throughout her discourse, Lovejoy defines *representation* as "a form of ideology because it has inscribed within it all the attitudes we have about our response to images and their assimilation; and about art making in general, with all its hierarchies of meaning and intentionality" (p.14). As the tools available to artists change, so will the artists' perceptions of the roles of representation when producing objects, images, and new forms of visual communication. New questions relating to how artists straddle physical and virtual worlds, what work is yet to be done, and how artists will perform that work (p.14), are emerging as the role of artists as makers is reconfigured in this digital era. As a culture tied to technology, artists must be alert to the ways in which skepticism can "obscure the genuine aesthetic and cultural opportunities currently available" some of which may be presented as new ways of working and new artistic genres based on possibilities offered in cyberspace along with other digital modes of cultural production (Lévy, 2001:198).

While skepticism is inhibiting to the potential of new forms of mark making for image production, questioning artists' emergent approaches to using computers and digital programs can be useful. Some art education theorists, including Roland (1990) and Rogers (1995), suggest that art practitioners need to change their thinking about approaches to image making and production that utilize paintbox simulating software. Concerns are greatest when old forms of thinking about art making are simply superimposed over the new forms that are emerging (Elkins 2001). Roland in particular warns against using the computer as an extension of older models of making art. These cautions warrant both artists and art educators to rethink how images are created, manipulated, reproduced, and even disseminated using technology. The project of rethinking how art and images can be produced jointly by hand and by computer is a major concern of mine and other researcher/practitioners such as Paul Coldwell (2001) of Chelsea School of Art and Design in London.

Articulating the production and development of art works and images in a digital context requires new vocabularies for discussing visual qualities and developmental procedures that do not originate in traditional handmade art practices. These new vocabularies must also be adopted for use in the discipline of art education (Keifer-Boyd 1996). The current language base used to describe visual properties of handmade works must be reconstructed (not just reworded) in order to serve the new possibilities that emerge from the pixilization, manipulation and multiplication of imagery (Johnson 1996). Listening to the ways in which artists describe the exchanges of working by hand and by computer can provide important cues of how these new vocabularies might be structured.

While there is a great deal of information encoded in the physical property/surface of the traditional handmade work, the computer-produced digital image has a wide range of capabilities which "afford[s] interaction between and within mediums," which is not easily realized using traditional approaches to art making (Johnson 1996:184). However, many individuals including scientists and artists often try to preserve older models of creative expression with which they are familiar and with which they already have a comfortable language base to describe these forms. Often these descriptions are still based on an aesthetics that is grounded on white paper, paint and canvas, not a computer screen (Nadin, 1989 cited in Johnson, 1996:185). Johnson contends that in order to understand computer-produced and pixilated images, we must reassess "traditional terms and definitions for visual features" (p.192). A great deal of this reassessment must also deal with the dynamics of movement, a new virtual mobility that results in manipulation, multiplication, and dissemination at levels that have not been realized before with traditional handmade production.

## Creating openings for new perspectives

Reviewing the historical paths of skepticism that have often clouded the introduction of new technologies into already established procedures is important for developing an understanding of how artists are beginning to embrace yet another way of making into their practices. As I have already pointed out, adopting new technologies is not without varying degrees of hesitance and even resistance as it often involves rethinking practices that have become comfortable and familiar, developing new vocabularies, and shifting the way artists think about what it means to produce images of our culture. This also means recognizing technology as poi sis, a process of revealing rather than merely an instrumental means to an end. Most important in all of this is re-viewing the ways in which artists develop exchanges between and across various media forms, making connections between older and newer media thereby providing insight into how the machines are affecting the artists and how they see these new influences on their practices as advantageous or otherwise.

The conceptual lenses I have offered in this chapter provide particular ways of looking at different variables that affect artists' approaches to image making in both physical and virtual worlds. Questions regarding the various factors that are influencing the artists' choices to incorporate computers with their manual ways of producing images have emerged as an important focus of my investigation. The conceptual lenses present perspectives to be considered during the course of reviewing and discussing the testimonies of the six artists that follow in chapters 3 and 4. I offer these perspectives, not as absolute, inclusive, and incontestable, but rather as ideas that are impinging on my explorations into the ways artists make art and how the making is reconfigured as the artists' technologies change. The conceptual lenses I have described in this chapter provide a context for listening to the stories outlined in chapter three. The themes highlighted in chapter four have been extracted from the artists' conversations in relation to the theoretical frameworks I am building, and create yet another set of lenses for exploring the ways in which artists are using their computers in conjunction with manual art making procedures. These additional lenses are further employed in the process of developing new theories about the integration of computers within Fine Art practice.

# CHAPTER THREE: MICRO CASE STUDIES OF SIX VISUAL ARTISTS

## Positioning the artists' stories within a larger research context

My examination of the ways in which artists are incorporating the use of their home computers with their manual art making procedures, involves the testimonies of six particular working artists. Their testimonies provide a rich pool of information that enables an exploration of the relations of exchange and integration that occur through real and virtual interchanges. The artists describe their disruptions, challenges, frustrations and triumphs as they recount their experiences during engagements with computer technologies. The six artists are all varied individuals whose art making practices are quite different from each other. Their variances allow similarities, differences, and contradictions to surface within and between their stories because of such factors as age, career experience, work habits, and home/studio/family situations. All of the artists have begun to integrate the use of their home computers in varying capacities with their art production over the last three years.

The micro case studies play an important role within the larger research project of this book. I am adamant that listening to different artists' perceptions as they recount their experiences regarding the provocations, the obstacles, and the discoveries inherent in integrating new media forms with old practices is crucial to understanding how new technologies impose themselves on our living and working routines. Furthermore, it is essential to hear stories from the front line so to speak, before developing new theories, or at worst, re-propagating old assumptions. The artists' own words provide an excavation site into the implications of merging old ways of working manually with new ways of working digitally, offering glimpses of challenges and disruptions that are happening across disciplines and cultural contexts. Their testimonies provide insight into individuals whose work offers new ways of reading our culture.

It is also my intention to position the work of artists in general, which includes the procedures and processes that make up their practices, via a form of qualitative inquiry.

Just as field work is the primary method for collecting qualitative research data which finds its form in life histories, autobiographies, case studies, letters, open interviews and participant observation (Jacob 1987), research and documentation that is part of the art making process spawns qualitative data in the form of artist statements, essays, studio journals and diaries (Stout 1999). The artist uses these forms of data to identify themes and construct new theories about the multiple ways in which the world can be viewed and experienced. The artist as researcher collects bits of information and pieces of cultural matter, experimenting with various juxtapositions as a way of forming a bricolage of images, text, and sound (Denzin & Lincoln 1994; Kearney 1988). Through these juxtapositions artists develop new relationships and themes in their quest to construct new meaning and alternative perspectives. As Watrin suggests, the "qualitative work of artists is fraught with inventions, creations, and resolutions that shift existing boundaries" (1999:93).

Watrin romantically defines the artist as a kind of researcher. She contends that artists' explore and study their subjects within their own particular settings or contexts, demarcating specific events, interactions, and exchanges through rich description whether that is visual, textual or aural. She maintains that "artists thoroughly immerse themselves in the phenomenon they wish to interpret and understand" (1999:95). However, in an effort to break down romantic notions of the artist as autonomous creator, I would also contend that the artist does not immerse themselves in their research in ways that prohibit the effects of social relations and exchanges, but rather acknowledges these effects as inevitable in shaping and shifting the boundaries of their inquiry.

Art making is an activity that generates diverse views and perspectives on how individuals see the world as it is, or as importantly, on how it could be (Greene 2000). In light of this potential, the occasion to study the ways that artists research and develop ideas for making art provides opportunities to examine variations in their research and development processes as they work with different media under a variety of conditions. In a way, I am the researcher who is studying the processes of other researchers within a shared domain. What I have drawn from researching these particular six artists' working practices are the ways in which they contest and rethink existing forms of representation and production and "bring ideas into society that might not yet be visible" (Becker 2002:19). As the artists discuss their procedures for research and production, moments arise when they appear to contradict themselves. These moments highlight various conflicts inherent in working across different modalities. Through the variations, aporias, silences, and disruptions in their stories, the artists offer glimpses of "what might be . . . what should be, and what is not yet" (Greene 2000:19). The six artists' testimonies provide a starting point from which to discuss the contests and conundrums that surface for artists who are using computers to research and produce imagery in their still mostly manual practices.

Listening to the voices of artists grappling with such issues must be considered as part of the inquiry process and integral to understanding the phenomenon of working concurrently by hand and computer. In turn, the research relies heavily on the artists' perceptions of how they investigate their ideas, and to what degree they see their art making processes and production affected by virtual contexts of digital culture, for example through programs such as Photoshop and communications technologies like the Web. The artists are required to tap into their imaginations and closely examine how they work, ask questions of themselves and "be present-from their own perspectives" (Greene 2000:34).

**Why these artists?**

Two main criteria for selection became evident when deciding who should participate. Each artist chosen would be engaged in traditional two dimensional, mark-making art processes such as painting or drawing using conventional art materials and media and have started incorporating home computers into their manual ways of working. They would also be avid Web surfers and navigators, accessing the Internet for information and communication purposes on a regular, almost daily basis. All of the artists reside and work within the Hamilton and Greater Toronto area in art communities that I myself have been a part of, and thus I am familiar with their social, political and cultural contexts. The artists represent emergent, mid career and senior level artists.

All of the artists I interviewed for this study have established practices that involve an ongoing commitment to communicating ideas and concepts through the "handmade" production of art objects. The reason for selecting artists who use traditional art making processes is to examine how their ideas and concepts are formed across varying media domains. Particularly interesting here is the crossover between analog, handmade procedures and digital media forms which position artists within both physical and virtual contexts when making. These crossovers include engagements with the information excessive domains of the Web. As Collins suggests, research needs to consider how high tech access to excessive information domains like the Web are affecting "anachronistic low tech" forms of cultural production (1995:6). Such research also highlights the ways in which artists construct new aspects of self as they negotiate a multiplicity of physical and virtual territories.

The artists' testimonies bring forward the terms on which they recognize the crossovers they are making in the process of integrating and exchanging different strategies of production across domains, employing diverse selves across a variety of social and historically influenced conditions. Articulating their experiences during the interviews provided an opportunity for them to see, on several levels, the disruptions and challenges that displace their grounded sense of self from one context, and place it in another, possibly unfamiliar location or space. The ways in which the different artists deal with this displacement and reconfiguration of space lend important insight to the issues of moving across physical and virtual worlds and living out the challenges imposed by new technologies.

With these considerations of both displacement and reconfiguration in mind, inviting artists from a wide range of career experience and age provides the opportunity to explore Negroponte's (1995) claims that the challenges we all face, and the stories we all tell in relation to *becoming digital,* are generationally based. This claim becomes more evident as the artists' describe their different ways of coming to use computers both in their daily living routines, in their art practice, and any initial scepticism that accompanied this development.

The artists for the micro studies were also chosen with distinct characteristics in mind with regard to their approaches and assumptions about art practice. One of the artists, Peter, is well established and has been so for many years. He has had a number of exhibitions in both anglo and francophone communities so he is well versed in changing language contexts. Another of the senior artists, Claire, seems to be in a continual process of re-emerging. Claire has had several exhibitions over the past few years, but does not exhibit as regularly as Peter, yet thinks about her art making all the time. Her comfort level in the studio is much different than Peter's in that she acts as though "the studio" is a place that is loaded with all sorts of assumptions about working and producing "good art." Donna, the third artist in the senior category, is still learning about art making and has limited exhibition experience. She has attained a high level of comfort in the studio and continuously mixes her production activities with other daily events in her home which physically surrounds her studio. Donna also likes to categorize things, such as the way she uses her computer. She likes clean and distinct boundaries between its different capabilities. Claire on the other hand relishes the crossovers and the opportunity to blur the boundaries.

Negroponte (1995) maintains that becoming digital is generationally affected. I have purposely chosen a dichotomy of younger and older artists to interview for this study. The younger artists, Robyn, Jin and Jack, were all introduced to computers during the developmental stages of their practices at art college. Their knowledge about image production has been informed by computer-based technologies and digital imaging procedures even though none of the three has chosen to develop practices that privilege computer technologies over handmade methods. In contrast to this, the three older artists learned about computers through other daily activities and began considering their use as a new way of working long after they had established a practice based on manual procedures, although Donna's development began later and had the potential to be affected by computers at that time.

Among the three younger artists, Jack is different in his thinking. He is more like an older artist in his approach to painting due in part to his modernist perceptions of art making. He is very much influenced by the Abstract Expressionists and appreciates the surfaces he creates in his work. He comes from a family who, through different trades, has worked with their hands all their lives. Jin and Robyn however, are very much engrossed with the Web and their abilities to be "virtually mobile" across the globe. While they appreciate handmade work and processes, they are enamored by the popular cultural tendencies of the Web, and the *slickness* of presentation. Like Jack, Jin describes his ties to family heritage. Jin is Korean. His ties to the Korean culture are realized through his imagery, while Jack's ties to family emerge through his painting technique. Robyn on the other hand is trying to carve out her own niche as a young artist working in a vibrant urban culture. Her influences are magazine and advertising images stimulated by the desires and consumer savvy (fashion, home decor etc.) that she sees attributed to her generation.

The diversity of the study artists provides an opportunity to bring out the differences in aesthetic sensibilities, variations in comfort levels in the studio, similarities and discrepancies in assumptions about art and image production, and most obviously, to highlight generationally-based issues. While all six artists value the handmade attributes of their practices, some value their computer exchanges more than others. The ease with which they spoke about their practices, their commitment to making work regardless of how it is accepted in the larger art world, and their contention (for now) that they will always make work that lives in the physical world of tactile sensation have made these artists valuable contributors to this study. Their willingness to divulge their challenges and apprehensions opens up a variety of issues and questions concerned with moving across physical and virtual contexts in art and image production.

## Commencing the conversations

Each artist completed an online survey, was interviewed once in person and then contacted several times by email to clarify statements they made or asked additional questions to aid my analysis. The topics of the interview questions that I posed to all the artists focus on their experiences of integrating computer technologies into their mostly handmade, manual ways of producing images and making art. The artists' stories have developed from the conversations that took place during individual, face-to-face interviews that were tape recorded. Twenty-five questions were posed in the same order to each artist (see Appendix A). The semi-structuredness of the interviews facilitated an open conversation enabling spontaneous questions to be introduced by either myself, (the interviewer) or the artists. Lasting about 60 to 90 minutes, some of the conversations took place at the artists' studios allowing me a glimpse of their working spaces, while other interviews were conducted at their work places or their homes. I asked each artist to select a location that was most convenient and comfortable for them.

Before each artist was interviewed, they answered a 12-question survey by email (Appendix B) where they introduced their art making beginnings and provided demographic information such as: how much time do they spend making art, how much time using a computer, the placement of their computer in relation to their studios and the type of Internet connection they use. The issues discussed with each artist include: how they approach the exploration and development of ideas, how they use the Web to research those ideas, how they develop their ideas into visual representations, how they integrate digital processes into their manual approach to art making, how they have adapted to the constant change and innovation offered by digital technologies, and the experiences they recognize as important in shaping their practices.

Each interview was tape recorded and transcribed verbatim. Using the artists' own words to illustrate the various issues and themes put forward is very important to the texture of the ensuing discussion, and crucial as well to new theories that emerged during my analysis. Field notes describing the interview environment accompanied each tape, providing me with a setting for examining these discussions. The artists were asked to answer each question as it pertained to their own situations and they were invited to elaborate on any area of discussion that they felt was important to understanding their perspectives on the issues.

The interview questions were designed to allow maximum opportunity for the artists to tell their stories while seeing themselves as "persons in process" (Greene 2000:41). Many of the artists claimed at the end of the interviews that hearing their own words put a voice to their processes in ways that enabled them to see the procedures they adopt for making art. Before the interviews, they had not considered the ways in which they negotiated different terrains and how who they are as artists are affected by these negotiations. If art making is perceived as a way of becoming for these artists, then our conversations became in part an articulation of those processes of becoming.

## Presenting the artists: My initial analysis of their stories

*I'm intrigued by computer-based work a little bit, almost like somebody's intrigued by an accident (Claire).*

Quoting the participants in their own words and emphasizing their voices is crucial to the understanding of their reality. In addition to considering the social relationships that effect the ways in which individuals construct meaning, *voice* suggests the distinct relationship each artist enters into as she/he continue to construct and reconstitute meaning. The remainder of this chapter focuses on presenting the six artists who constitute the micro case studies by way of my initial analysis of their conversations. The introductions present the artists in relation to who they are and how they see themselves as makers and producers of images. The criteria for extracting dialogue from the transcribed interviews for these introductions are predicated on descriptions of how each artist develops ideas for making art and their relationship to computer technologies within the context of exploring these ideas. I have used pseudonyms when referring to the artists in this book.

**Peter**

Peter is a 53-year-old mixed media artist working in drawing, collage, and gouache, who maintains a studio in a warehouse district of Toronto as well as working at home. He presents his work through artist-run centres, many of which are francophone. Peter spends several hours a day using a computer for email, graphic design, administration for his own art career, and web site design, even though he does not have his own web site as yet. Peter's computer is located at home, separating its use and location from the studio where he creates his hand-drawn graphite works. Part of the reason for this is that Peter's studio is in a warehouse which he claims may be too dusty to house a computer, yet it is also where he keeps most of his drawings. It is interesting to note that Peter's computer is still in a similar location as it was when he was first introduced to this technology. It still has a multipurpose function within the family and is site-specific to Peter's domestic space rather than being integrated into his art making space. The particular locations of technologies are affected by the social relations and processes that are inherent in that location. The technologies also spawn new relations between their particular functions and their interchanges with everyday living and working routines. Peter's computer is not located within the space he uses for his more physical forms of art making. The interview with Peter took place in his studio with his large scale black and white graphite drawings on paper as the backdrop. The studio is a site for handmade production.

Peter gleans ideas for his art making from language and text. He works out many of his ideas in sketch books which have a material relationship to the "hand-held" reading and reference books he collects and is so attached to, claiming that it was through books that he discovered new things, places and people while growing up. He researches ideas through reading books and through making numerous notes and small illustrations in note books. They are his way of developing ideas. He asserts that it is the *marked page* that is important to him. It maintains his connection to language which is so important to his ideas and ensuing creative practice. As Peter is a former archeologist, he compares his own sketch books to artifacts that represent some form of historical narrative. He sees his books as relating to particular periods in his life, and they are implicated in the cultural codes that were significant at the time the images were developed and the books were used. Peter suggested that his way of exploring image production was also analogous to walking into a smoke-filled room. "You know that there is a door on the other side, but where, you are not quite sure. You know you'll get to it eventually." Again, he related this sensation to archeological processes of excavating and discovery.

Peter says he works intuitively. "I think I'm a person who's very sensual. I really react very strongly to the information my senses provide me." He maintains that he "feel[s] things more than sort of knows what they are." Yet, on the other hand, Peter does a great amount of research in the process of developing his work. He has an affinity to using printed matter and books for his research and contends that this comes from his formative years and his love for books and reliance on them as a source of enjoyment and learning. He states, however, that although he now uses the Web for a lot of his researching instead of venturing out to the local library, he does not view the Web as a text-based system.

> Some of my problems with the web are largely a part of the fact that it is not being well used. I think it has tremendous potential - it fascinates me, but I'm not always convinced that the way the information is presented is necessarily the best way for it to be useful. So I think in some respects we actually build barriers to communicating on the web because we do not understand the way it is as an education place.

Interestingly, Peter contradicts his statement later in the conversation by saying,

> By and large, the Web is still very text based which is fine by me, because I'm a text based person and I'm also very interested in the letter form in typography. So, the way it looks as well as it is a vehicle for information, but unfortunately I don't think that is where we are going. I think it's more of a movie/television kind of frame that we're heading for. How I'll fit into that I don't know because I'm basically not a dynamic image person. I'm a static image person, so it'll be interesting to see how people like me fit into that and how the written word will accommodate that.

It appears that Peter is in flux over his relationship with the Web and the ways in which he can best utilize Web-based resources for researching and art making. He realizes that there is an unrealized potential for what can be done, but he is not sure, and a little skeptical as to whether this new modality will be sympathetic to older ways of making and viewing images. He hesitates to predict whether his way of perceiving and making images will fit with Web ways of representing the world.

Furthermore, Peter is conscious of his age in relation to emerging technologies, believing that "society has sort of been divided into two camps. There are people who are born into technology" who have "a different way of working" than he does. He actually makes this point four times during the interview, confirming Negroponte's claims of generational-based digital-ness.

> I'm part of a generation that has a foot in two camps. So those people who don't, who see it as being something alarming, or horrendously complex and not something they want to delve into. There are those who are interested in it, but most of the people I know are people who were not born with the computer, so I think that's something that's really important to know. It is a complex tool and I think somebody coming into it - I think it can be quite daunting regardless of our gooey interfaces and everything that will make it easier. I don't think it is necessarily the easiest thing to deal with. Interestingly enough, I was sort of dragged kicking and screaming into the computer age. I had no interest. I couldn't see why I would be interested in exploring it at all, which, looking back on it right now, seems odd coming from an artist where you imagine that artists are curious about everything . . . completely seduced by it . . . I was so amazed by the ease that [I] got into it that I became totally addicted to it.

As one of the senior members of the interview group, Peter claims he has "a schizophrenic existence as an artist" because he had not completely moved into computer-based ways of working.

> There is a certain remoteness to it which fascinates me and frustrates me. I can work for hours on something and I lose a sense of time and scale and for whatever reason the work does not give me the physical satisfaction that I get coming into the studio and using a brush or a pencil. Has it really extinguished my enthusiasm for the technology? It hasn't convinced me that it's going to be a prime tool in my creative process, but it's becoming increasingly important.

Peter explained that creating his large scale work is "more satisfying physiologically, than the computer technology," yet he still expressed excitement and fascination by the possibilities of using computers in the course of developing images. The physical tactility of art production and satisfaction gained from its processes is strongly tied to Peter's studio space which is separate and at a distance from his home. Integrating the computer more readily into his working procedures is complicated and quite possibly inhibited by Peter's decision to keep his computer at home in a space separate from his manual production. In this way, Peter determines a form of site-specificity for his computer that is removed from the space where he performs physical acts of pleasure through art making. Tactility and place become the powers at stake for Peter in his integration of computer technology into his art making practice.

Returning to Peter's thoughts about using the Web, he describes his most contentious issues as prejudiced by our education system, which he feels fails to recognize the need for content in what we communicate and teach. Peter is also a college instructor.

> Content is something - that we lack, the greatest problem we face in North America, in Canada and in Toronto is in the education system, we do not address the problem of content. The education system deals with the tools. It deals with the structure. It does not deal with content. For 5 years I taught in a community college and basically I was always being told that you have to teach them "photo shop" you have to teach them how to use the computer. And I said you have to learn about typography, you have to learn about colour, you've got to learn about design, you've got to learn about writing for the Web.

Peter is frustrated that the Web has such a great potential for delivering content in interactive forms and providing rich experiences, but that it simply isn't there yet. Instead he complains, it still thinks one-dimensionally in relation to Disney style entertainment rather than thinking pedagogically about how the content is transferred to the Web user.

> I'll see things and I can't get close enough to them because we're still locked into a book format where someone will put up on a Web site an image of say a sculpture - a Henry Moore and my reaction would be - Oh I can turn this and walk around this virtually, I can get up close and actually look at the metal, I could reference how it is built and all of a sudden you realize, no - all you have is one slide that has been digitized and put on the Web. So in some cases, the potential of the Web is not being realized. What could be said about the Henry Moore - isn't there. So I'm often times frustrated by what I perceive as being the way I could really access something and seeing its limitations.

Peter critiques the Web from two particular viewpoints. The first being the lack of seeing the Web's full potential as an interactive and collaborative learning environment and secondly, the lack of in-depth content of what is available. He suggests that structure and technical information supplant the potential for real and useful content. As well, the corporate and individual interests that are driving the Web are all tied to money and expense which is why individuals such as artists and other public intellectuals are limited in their abilities to explore the Web's potential. He contends that artists could really make inroads into the potential capabilities of the Web as they have the ability to see things as they could be without corporate overtones.

In several instances Peter relayed feelings of apprehension about our culture's current understanding of the potential of computer technology.

> I'm not sure that we've found the voice of computer technology. For the most part we're not really using its potential. The things that I'm doing are analogous in the archeological record of human kind in that what I'm doing, is I've taken what I've done elsewhere and trying to see how it adapts to the digital world.

It appears that Peter is trying to superimpose the methods (*cf.* Elkins 2001) he employs for manual art making to new ways of working digitally. He compares his way of adapting methods with what he sees has happened historically in the discovery of new ways of material production. Newer methods are superimposed over older methods with the hope that there will be a successful blending of procedures. In this way he illustrates Roger's (1995) and Roland's (1990) concerns of unabashedly imposing one media form on another without regard for the specificity or incompatibility of procedures. While acknowledging that superimposing new procedures over old may not lead to a successful undertaking for artists, Peter has not altogether seen ways beyond this process. While he has stated many times there are new opportunities for producing images and content, he himself has not fully taken up the task of developing that potential. However, Peter did suggest that computer technology allows him to see his body of work as a whole. The change in scale from large room-sized installations, too big to fit his studio space all together, is seen anew on a smaller scale via the computer screen. This affords Peter the opportunity to rethink his physical relationship to his work and the power relations he has imposed on the spaces where it is housed.

> In the case of my own work, I think, what it [the computer] does, again is related to the scale at which I work. It allows me to see things I ordinarily can only in the rarest of exhibitions where there's wall space that's extensive enough to allow me to put up several pieces. Basically, we're here in a space now where I have two works up and ordinarily, other spaces I've worked in, I've had space for one or only portions of a piece, so the Web [via a personal web page] allows me to look through my life's work in a way that would be very difficult otherwise. It would allow me to do it in a way that would never happen in my lifetime. I can't imagine a book being done on my life's work, but I could assemble those images and throw them up on the Web on a site or something without a great deal of difficulty.

The new virtual presentation space focuses on the scale and the breadth of Peter's work as it represents his life as an artist, rather than the physicality of individual pieces. In regards to his relationship with computer technology, Peter described his initial engagement as,

> something that was a parallel stream of exploration. It didn't seem to be integrated, it tended to be a support, it was a tool. I used it for administration, for putting together information to circulate and so forth, and little bit by little bit, I started trying to use it in my image making process, but I tended to use it in a very limited way, copying, pasting, things like that and sort of in comparison perhaps to what I'd seen other people do with the technology. It always seemed to me that I was using it in a very - like what I said - I had my foot in both camps. I felt a little uncomfortable with the face that I would be presenting as being computer-based when I haven't really figured out how I can use what I do in a Web way that will give me the satisfaction in saying that I'm actually communicating something to people.

Peter claims that he *had* his foot in two camps, suggesting that he has now moved on to a new position that is more comfortable and workable. Peter appears to know his situation very well and is quite computer savvy. He uses a computer for both producing images and viewing a body of his work in its entirety. However, I would also like to suggest that Peter still needs to feel some kind of physical connection to the work that enables him to see its communicative value. When that connection is missing, or possibly changed its form, Peter is unsure if the communicative link may also be missing. When asked if he could ever see his art making become completely computer or web-based, he suggested,

> It's difficult because the Web is customizable or the way you access it is customizable by the individual who uses it, so it's a very interesting situation in terms of - I guess I'll approach it from my experience as a Web designer. It can be extremely frustrating because you have very little control over how people will see what you do. A lot of that has to do with bandwidth. You are limited by the technology and what you can throw up. So the compromises you have to make, puts you into a creative space that sometimes is very difficult to deal with because ultimately, what you put

> out there isn't anywhere close to what you originally intended. On the other hand, for someone like myself who is involved with static imagery, possibly that would push me in a direction that could be very interesting. In essence, what is it I want to do, and what is the minimum requirement for me to do that? That is not something that is foreign to me. The way I work tends to be reductionist, a way of simplifying everything so that doesn't strike me as being totally foreign to the way I work. What's not obvious is exactly what common denominators are the tools of your expression? It's a challenge for sure.

It seems that Peter has thought a great deal about his work in digital contexts, and has used computer programs to some extent in his procedures. He still wants to delineate the two modalities for working and maintains a physical distance between the space he uses for manual production and the place where his computer is located. There are many practical reasons for this separation, one which he mentioned as the suitability of the warehouse space for safely housing the computer, the other is financial resources in that he cannot afford two computers. Peter himself however, propagates that separation through his assumptions about the Web and how it is used. He is suspicious as to whether or not he can communicate on an unfamiliar and mutable ground. He contends that there should be obvious common denominators that distinguish an artist's form of expression and presentation. Moving the production and presentation of one's work to a mutable media form such as the Web, interrupts the ability to maintain these apparently recognizable features blurring the distinctions and boundaries between them.

There are risks inherent in blurring the boundaries and unfixing familiar ways of working, possibly losing sight of one's original direction, and in this case, the image, in the process. The underlying premise of exploring new contexts and modalities is the understanding that in order to discover the new, one must "take the risk of getting lost" along the way, diverting from familiar practices (Burbules, 2000:181; Lévy 2001:67). This particular feeling of being lost, of not being sure which way to go next, is defined by Burbules as "aporia: a problem of having arrived in an unfamiliar location" (2000:172). In Peter's case, the Web presents a site that is unfixed and unattached from his familiar practices of developing and presenting images. He is still grappling with the possibility of losing sight of the common denominators that distinguish his work, even at the expense of finding a new direction. As for long term repercussions of exchanging physical and virtual modalities in the process of producing and disseminating images, Peter claims: "I'm not sure that I really know. I'm living it so I don't have a way of distancing myself from it so it's really difficult to comment." However, as for the role of artists in this new digital era, Peter is quite certain that "we are the specialists in content." I interpret this to mean that Peter views artists as expert meaning makers who offer cultural barometers from which the rest of society can gauge itself.

**Claire**

Claire is a 53-year-old mixed media artist who has a passion for drawing. I met with Claire in her living room, in the home she shares with her husband. I have personally known Claire for about 15 years and have exhibited with her as part of an artists' collective. Her living room has a great deal of light coming through, more so than her studio which is in the basement. I have not seen this new studio, it is Claire's sanctuary, not because she hasn't made her working spaces more public before, but this space always appears to me as different, more personal, more hidden. We began the interview with the same question I had asked the other participants: Where do you get your ideas for making art? For Claire and me however, this is a question we have talked around many times in our endless discussions on being artists, but we have never tried to answer the question directly.

When the interview was formally completed, Claire mentioned that she felt drained and tired, but at the same time exhilarated. It had been a reflective process for her and she said that she could actually hear herself giving the answers and as was evident in some of the pauses in the conversation, she was trying to listen to what she was saying. She exuded a great deal of passion in her answers and like many others in this process got particularly passionate about the importance of *the hand* and her handmade processes relating to the pieces she was creating. She had not considered a lot of the questions I was asking before and admitted that they seemed important to reflect on in order that she sees her own working processes. It was important for her to hear her own words - to hear her own voice.

Claire contends that she is "a storyteller that doesn't write." Her whole creative process that leads to her making is related to the constant recording of experiences on bits of paper and reinterpreting those recordings through other recordings:

> when I'm working on those bits of paper it's just at that moment, for me that's a conduit for getting it [the idea] inside of me and when it's in there and all of those different things that I've collected over maybe 5 years are bubbling around.

Claire' forms of recordings are note taking and mark making. She is extremely passionate about drawing, "by itself it has a language and expression capability that nothing else does . . . Other peoples' reactions to drawing is that it is a means to an end rather than a pursuit by itself." The ideas that contribute to Claire's art making come from a diversity of sources, but most important, they evolve from everyday life and in particular, the "cross references and cross pollinations" of the very small things that almost go unconsidered. Choosing to reinterpret the everyday has an established background in Dutch painting and can be seen in the work of Vermeer and van Eyck. These artists chose to focus in on and emphasize the details of the ordinary, reflecting domestic interiors and everyday functions and chores of ordinary individuals. The ordinary life routines are depicted in ways that call our attention to these forms of everydayness.

Lefebvre suggests that the everyday become the common denominator amongst different sets of functions that appear to be distinct systems, but through a sense of "everydayness" they retain connections with each other (1987:34). Reinterpreting the everyday has been the focus of many Pop artists, not only through their work, but also through such acts as Rauchenberg and Warhol's attending to the everydayness that came into their studios via a television that was always turned on (Farmer 2000). In Claire's case, however, it is the act of documenting fragments of ordinary events, focusing in on details that might otherwise go unnoticed that is important.

> I always travel with a note pad and I have a palm pilot . . . it is beside my bed or in my purse. I have a note pad there in case the palm pilot fails, and on my desk I have a note pad and in my studio I have a note pad, so I always carry paper because, for example, I'll be sitting in a movie and I'll write a quote down . . . I keep shovelling in things and then eventually they come to the surface joined with something else that has been shovelled in there . . . It's like collecting pieces of a puzzle that ends up forming itself in the end.

This information gathering becomes the catalyst to her coming to the process of making.

> I gather like crazy and then there comes a point where I can feel an urgency, I can feel it coming and then I have to go to the studio. Then I nest like crazy and then it depends on how afraid I am of the idea how much I have to nest. Being afraid of the idea means I think I'm always afraid whether I'll do something justice because I think if I've stumbled on to something I think is important, I'd like to express, I don't want to cheapen it, I don't want to marginalise it, I really want it, I really need to find a way for it to go directly to the soul and then to the intellect so

people will be kind of impacted by it on some level and then examine it.

Claire is currently gathering emails that have been forwarded to her by a variety of people for a variety of reasons. This new process of collecting and archiving has inspired content for making artists' books.

Claire's cultural background has an underlying effect on how she interprets the everyday and approaches the world and interprets her experiences. Claire views the "real world" and the "computer world" like they are two distinct cultures. It appears that working between two contexts at any given time is part of Claire's way of being an artist.

> I think definitely the German cultural thing influences me a lot. I want to make things that directly engage the things that I hold between the two cultures and how my first culture informs where I am in this culture, but there's a lot of work like that being done out there, so I don't want to be just another person exploring their roots so it's in there all the time and I think subconsciously it affects what I do anyway and directly. I'm always searching for . . . someday I will find a way of expressing it.

Claire also looks to film, music, literature, and the media to find and document samples of everydayness. She seeks out these fragments by opening up her routines to the possibility of discovering something new or rethinking what currently exists.

> When I get a book in my hands then I'm compelled to go get a pencil because the book requires that from me, not because I sit down and I say okay I'm going to read a book so now I have to get a piece of paper, but because the book says after so many pages that if you don't get a pencil you're going to miss something absolutely amazing. I'll be writing those things down and that then influences my work . . . I have kept many newspaper clippings in my file to inspire me . . . what I will look for in those clippings are the very human qualities, the microcosms in an

> individual life that makes that large expression almost understandable or know where the seeds of that large expression comes from.

Claire's art making practice is based on reconceptualizing the experiences she has of encountering everyday life from a variety of influences and sources and mixing these experiences together to form new relationships and meanings. She is very much an "active interpreter" of the journey that she has embarked on as an artist which has enabled her to "turn back upon [her] own texts and see there [her] own processes and biases of selection at work" (Grumet 1981a:141). Claire says "I'll get a certain distance along in the piece and then there's a communication coming back to me as I see what's coming out of me." This very process became evident during our interview. Claire began to describe how she uses a computer in relation to her subjectivity that is grounded in the role of a hand maker of art objects. As she spoke, she appeared to be fleshing out the ways she has been approaching art making as well as using her computer. As she begins to involve computer technologies in her art making practice, Claire is reevaluating the importance of her drawings and her own hand markings.

Claire's relationship with computer technology developed as a result of her returning to art school as a mature student. Her computer use was not related in any way to image production, but rather through writing essays. It functioned as an electronic typewriter that, while more efficient than old fashioned electric, table top versions, incurred more risk taking.

> I was computer phobic when I started years ago. It dropped an entire 30 page essay on me, never to be found again, and I had to start over. Where it dropped it was not in the research part, but in the thinking part, where it all got pulled together and it took a long time to build my confidence in that thing again.

Claire's confidence returned as she became reliant on the computer when she developed a small consulting business. Now she claims,

> I think on the computer, like I actually sit down and think and work on it while I'm thinking . . . Certainly the computer has already become one of the tools that I use to make a piece of work, but more in the literal sense.

Claire's comfort level is still tied to the particular function of the computer. In most of her engagements she is performing tasks that have some connection to older ways of working such as typing essays or cataloguing information in an electronic notepad. The challenge arises however when she deliberates about exchanging her manual practices of producing images with new mediated forms via the computer. She is intrigued by what could happen and the possibilities that arise, but is apprehensive of her compatibility with that way of thinking.

> I'm intrigued by computer-based work a little bit, almost like somebody's intrigued by an accident. It looks really interesting, but not to the point where I want to do it. The problem for me is that a lot of the work is generated quickly and I'm a very slow methodical thinking artist so I'm not sure that it's a good marriage for me.

The technology has a strong draw for Claire as she personifies its existence in her descriptions. However, she is cautious of this electronic being due to past encounters that left her stranded as was the case of her essay in school. She seems guarded about her art making practice in that she does not want to expose herself to producing works so quickly that she does not take time to consider all the options or the pitfalls of going in one particular direction over another. I interpret her concern as *things can happen before you know it without even thinking.* Claire needs time to reflect on her processes and computer programs are not always obliging.

Claire's relationship to computer technology is also influenced by her perception of age in relation to comfort level, stating that she feels younger artists may be more inclined to try new machines. This again refers to a perceived level of risk-taking that is involved in integrating new media into older established ways of working. Her concerns lie more with how older ways of working and new media will find their places and "fit" together in the art community.

> I sometimes feel a little bit concerned, and not out of anything I've heard or experienced, just emotionally, that there will no longer be room for the more traditional work and I would like it if there's room for both. I'm really intrigued by computer-based work. I like to look at it and learn more from it. I hope we don't throw out the baby with the bath water. I think for a time it might happen. When something new comes along, there is this blush of newness, this excitement and then everybody wants to be in on it. Then it takes its rightful place in the scheme of things taking a position in that culture with everything else. Then the balance is corrected again . . . taking a place with other forms of expression . . . I think artists like to think that they are nifty and special and in front of things . . . not that artists can necessarily influence directly what's happening in the world, but they certainly can mirror and I think they can be one of the influences of what is happening and how it is interpreted.

Claire's interest in what technologies can do for her own practice is somewhat guarded. While she likes the crossovers in the way she presents ideas through her work, she prefers that different modalities for working, in this case virtual and manual procedures, are kept separate. She does however, imply that all modalities should somehow complement each other and fit comfortably and democratically within the larger order of art world activity. She needs to see that both old and new ways of working find a balance. While Claire likes to look at the impact (the accident) of new technology through the work of others, she is hesitant to get closer through her own procedures, by getting her hands dirty so to speak.

Claire's romantically impressed perception of her role as an artist is to bring into dialogue text and images. Through this dialogue she intends

> . . . to invite people to examine stuff, whether it's the way they live their lives or it's the way they have opinions. It's to invite them to see something ordinary in a different way. I think to invite them to remember if they've forgotten or, to tell them, no, not to tell them. I used to think my job was to tell people stuff, but it isn't really. Maybe to mirror life, and to invite them to investigate how important and what an influence the little things have . . . I'm an information gatherer out in the world and when I'm in art making space I'm in an amalgamating, ingredient mixing kind of space, and when I'm in my studio I'm in flow. In flow you're really not conscious of anything because it's all coming through you . . . there's something about a wonderful merger or marriage or something, between your hands your heart and your head when they work together it's a really amazing thing.

Defining the various spaces where different parts of her art making process occur are integral to Claire's understanding of her processes. Just as she delineates the diverse modalities of making into older and newer patterns that are influenced by the surge of technology, her own procedures are delineated between spaces for researching, developing, and then the actual making. While some of these spaces are attached to notepads and material objects, other spaces are electronic and virtual. These ways of working are site-specific for Claire and tie her meaning making to particular procedures in particular places.

**Robyn**

Robyn is a 26-year-old art administration assistant and recent graduate of a four-year Bachelor of Fine Arts degree. Robyn does a variety of work including painting, drawing, computer-generated drawing, photography and installation. She has always wanted to be an artist which she confirmed through her decision to study art at a university, and strengthened during the creation of her thesis project during her last year of study. She designates spaces for art making wherever she happens to be living at a given time. At present she feels she is in a transitory stage, thinking about work, but trying to make a space for herself within her new shared living arrangements. She uses a computer daily for a variety of purposes including email, drawing, word processing, web page development and research. Robyn spends most of her time browsing and surfing the Web as well as working on her own web site that promotes her work.

The interview took place at Robyn's living space that she shares with three other artists. The space is a raw converted warehouse in the downtown core of Toronto. The space has been loosely divided into living and working areas. We were left alone by two departing roommates. We talked while the washing machine ran through its cycles and a cat ran through the living area. Robyn has some reservations about the space as it is not very large, the house-mates belongings tend to overlap each other, and there is an unfinished appearance to everything. Robyn suggested that she likes things fairly neat and organized and finished and this new (she has just been there a few months) living arrangement has been a challenge to her organized self. The location however, is very important to Robyn. Her work is influenced by the everydayness of the city. The converted warehouse where she lives is surrounded by a cacophony of urban activity and she can also walk just about anywhere that she needs to go.

Like Claire, Robyn's ideas for art making come from everyday life experiences, but they are often filtered through vehicles of popular culture, in particular the imagery found in fashion and interior design magazines. Her most current work has been inspired by Martha Stewart.

> I always loved magazines and as a teenager I always looked at Seventeen and all those magazines. I think photography initially was always really important to me so images, photographic images were always important. If you look through her [Martha Stewart's] magazines they are just gorgeous

> photographs, they have this really loaded up field, really soothing, muted colours . . . the way that things are composed, and the photographs are so gorgeous, I think that maybe, more than anything else because it wasn't the content, I wasn't reading her magazines, I was looking at them as visual candy. So I think I had all these magazines in my studio and my studio was immaculate and it could have been in a Martha Stewart magazine. . . I am really interested in decoration and the way we organize our space.

Lefebvre defines the everyday as a kind of product which "constitutes the platform upon which the bureaucratic society of controlled consumerism is erected" (1987:34). Martha Stewart's magazines use the everyday as an unwitting ideology, a totalizing subsystem of homogenizing style which can be purchased at many retailers. The everyday appear as the common denominator (and even part of the trademark) of Martha's own capitalist enterprise. Robyn uses the magazines, as a way to enter into these enterprises and comment on the simulacra of the images, and the power relations one can enter into when buying into this form of homogenous style. One way Robyn does this is through the use of language as part subject matter and part medium to present her ideas. She has been experimenting with anagrams, utilizing a website that helps her process her ideas as words, in particular reconstructing Martha Stewart's name as the branding insignia.

Robyn's computer usage is primarily through Web surfing. She began her web encounters while still at school.

> I saw it as sort of a break like I got to take a holiday from reading and doing projects for school and so I would sit at the computer and I would just surf. The first thing I would usually do is check my email and that might instigate going and looking up something I saw as interesting.

She is very comfortable surfing the Web even though she, like all the other artists, maintain that there is always a great deal of information to manage.

> The opportunity for finding information is greater now that we have the Internet. There's a lot more stuff you have to weed through, but sometimes it's really interesting.

There is a slight contradictory tone however to how Robyn describes her relationship to the Web. On the one hand, Web surfing requires a certain amount of effort to move through an abundant amount of information. This can be time consuming and frustrating, two common complaints by many individuals, including the artists who participated in this study. On the other hand, Robyn finds excitement in the potential discoveries that are only possible because of this weeding through process, and that would be less likely to happen if shortcuts to information sorting were more readily available. In light of this, I asked Robyn if she ever felt lost when surfing the Web. She said,

> I never feel lost, but some people might think that if they were in the same situation they'd feel lost. I just get so excited by anything that's new that it's like, okay, this may not have been what I had in mind, it's not what I was necessarily looking for, but this is interesting.

Robyn's position as an emerging artist affords her the easygoing posture that enables her to take risks. She is at a stage where everything new is a possible connection to drive her work forward. She doesn't have too many established ways of working that could be compromised by risk-taking and being led in new, unforeseen directions. She is actually searching out and embracing "what is new," and what things may influence her. She does not retain any resistance to computer technology or the Web, and lacks the skepticism that was evident, even if only in trace amounts, in the older artists.

Robyn enjoys the exploration and discovery aspect of Web surfing and has found a way of reconceptualizing the physical excitement by using the anagrams web site for composing her language-based works. It is a form of play, a form of game. As a very young, emerging artist, the Web has also presented Robyn with the opportunity to promote herself and her work at a distance. This reduces the risk of intimidation inherent in face-to-face contact with gallery owners as Robyn is able to assume the persona of a confident professional artist without the fear of in-person rejection.

> You can just send an email to the gallery and say I really want to send my stuff, when is your submission deadline, tell me about the gallery . . . I can be really outgoing and I can be shy too so it depends on how confident I'm feeling. I think the Internet helps people feel a little more comfortable because you're not on the phone or not in person sometimes so you can be yourself and not feel so nervous.

Robyn says she still needs to feel connected to the physical art community by attending openings and visiting galleries. Although she suggests that while email has opened up communication and, in particular, given the art community more mobility for sharing information and work, she believes that "people still need each other in a physical form . . . they still engage."

Robyn's connection to computer technology extends beyond the discovery mode inherent in web surfing. She is drawn to the organization of visual elements, cleanliness of line and form, and slick appearance of text and image presented by many web sites. It can be argued that these are properties also found in modernist style paintings and postmodern conceptual art such as the text-based work of Jenny Holtzer or Barbara Kruger. However, the aesthetic Robyn describes seems closer to the glossy Martha Stewart magazines she reads that present a particular middle class commercialized view of the urban environment. This slick aesthetic is also reinforced by the ever increasing sophistication of digital imaging capabilities in relation to higher degrees of screen and colour resolution and less evidence of pixilation. These properties still need a new language base for more distinct descriptions and critique in reference to image production and art making.

> I think that idea of cleanliness - everything being arranged in a very nice way, we've probably seen before the Internet, but it's something that I notice when I'm online. . . In terms of presenting my work it's always been really important to me to present my work in a professional way . . . I put it together so it looks super sleek and nice . . . I use a program so it all looks similar.

Robyn believes that using both computer technology and traditional media are issues of choice. She says that artists make choices all the time and to use computer technology or not is another choice. She herself has a relationship with the traditional medium of painting. She contends that the initial excitement over new media and the Web,

> . . . has died down a little bit and I don't think people are so afraid any more that it's [computer technologies and the Internet] going to take over and the traditional mediums will turn obsolete. More than ever, people want paintings or they want prints or they want something that is made by someone's hand using traditional tools. I think it's just a choice about who you are as an artist . . . we've all made choices whether technology is important in our art making . . . if you're a painter, I'm sure you still use email, you still go online, maybe it affects what you end up painting or maybe it doesn't . . . I think it affects some people and it doesn't affect others. I don't think you can draw a generalization.

As with all the other artists I conversed with, Robyn needs to leave her mark on the end product of her art making process. It is highly important that this mark be created by hand as a trace of her self within the process, or as Krauss submits, left as "a residue of its maker" (1993:151). The importance of these tracings runs across the artists' conversations of living both simultaneously through, and in between manual and digital processes of production. Robyn's love for images is both physical and virtual, and she has developed strategies for the two modalities to coexist within the research and production stages of her art making practice.

In regards to her role as an artist in the studio and an artist in cyberspace, Robyn says, "I'm not afraid to invite people to experience life in a different way. . what I try and do is just communicate. Artists open up peoples' minds to new ways of seeing and experiencing the world." As for her own Web site of work, "I've just sort of left it as a visual library so people can just kind of go through it and decide for themselves what's *going on there* . . . If you were to come to my studio I would open the door as if I would with my web site and I would show you around." Robyn appears to move easily between the physical and virtual spaces she uses for making art, regardless of her attachment to the materiality of the physical world.

**Jack**

Jack is a 28-year-old shipper/receiver at an art supply warehouse in downtown Toronto. He spends his time moving things around and working with his hands as part of his job. He has always wanted to be an artist since he was a child. He began his work in drawing and illustration using pencil, crayons and markers. He started painting when he went to art school in 1995. His studio is part of an old warehouse type of live/work space. His work is traditionally modern abstraction and he describes many of the early American abstract artists such as Jackson Pollock as his influences. Although he has not really liked how his work has been presented digitally in the past, he is still anxious to develop his own web site. We conducted the interview in a back corner of the warehouse at the end of the work day when the general activity was slowing down. Jack had already finished work. There were only a few interruptions and generally the flow of the interview was continuous.

Jack gathers his ideas for art making from the everydayness of his environment including the warehouse where he works.

> I find a lot of things here during the day will often influence what I do when I get home. Little nooks in the cardboard or a paint spill on the floor perhaps looking at someone else's art can spawn some ideas or definitely help with the creative process. I think it's an everyday thing that catches my eye. Cracks in the sidewalk actually are one of my favourites. Abstract aspects of those things - the abstract qualities and how they occur naturally. They're found everywhere, that's what is visually pleasing to me so it's things like that I pick up on.

Jack claims that his work just happens in a very spontaneous way without a great deal of planning or research:

> happy accidents on canvas, just letting chance play a big role, throwing paint down to see where it falls and maybe working a composition out of it . . . making mistakes . . . sort of living in the moment mentality I suppose, very spontaneous.

However, contrary to this spontaneous process, Jack has recently begun a new process that involves experimenting with computer renditions of colour that he finds through Web surfing. These digitized colour juxtapositions represent a new form of research and preparation which he perceives are becoming the foundation to his working process. The spontaneity becomes slightly subverted by the standardization inherent in the screen's pixelized colour combinations. Although he perceives his own making processes as mostly spontaneous creation, Jack has turned to the Web and computer programs such as Photoshop, to edit his apparently instinctive processes in the name of efficiency. The degree of intuition is contestable however, on the grounds that Jack has an established sense of aesthetics that has been influenced by many factors including art school and Abstract Expressionism.

> If I'm under a deadline or something and I really, really need to get this done . . . maybe wanting to use two colours and searching somewhere else [on the Web] to see how they would actually go together. It kind of contradicts what I said earlier about happy accidents. There's a time and a place for everything . . . before I used a computer, I really had no concept of how I could use it to my advantage. Now with programs such as Photoshop, just to divert for a second, I create a lot of work, again because I'm just sort of experimenting I really crank them [paintings] out. I've found now that I have a computer and I have some Photoshop techniques, I can create spontaneous paintings on the computer by the 10s and 20s and 30s within an hour and then maybe pick four or five of those ones that I would actually live with. It's like doing sketches . . . almost.

Using the computer has become a way of reducing the expense of wasted materials that could encumber his experimentation. While the computer experimentation lacks a large amount of physicality for Jack, the act of applying the paint during the later stages of making enables him to regain an important sense of physicality that is a crucial part of the work.

Jack is very conscious of how his young age contextualizes his experiences within digital culture. He questions his capacity for looking outside a world of computers and digitization.

> I'm sort of coming from a generation where I might not know otherwise [other than computerization]. I'm not coming right from the generation who was born on a lap top, but by grade five or six we started with the Commodore 64. I guess being at an age where you start to notice marketing, where you are out a little bit more and you're aware of what's happening and of your surroundings, I think I've just been part of the generation that's always been force-fed digital images . . . I definitely have to use my imagination to deal with what I might be looking at because I can understand that the translation of the actual piece or image to its state

> on the Internet changes because there are a lot of variables, so I try to imagine what it would look like in real life.

Jack's comments are interesting in that he does not see the computerization of image production as a way of extending his imagination as mentioned by some of the other artists. Instead, Jack claims that he must use his imagination to work back from the digitized images to visualize how they might appear in the material world. He has developed a strategy that enables him to move back and forth from digital to manual modes of image production translating the images as he moves. What is really interesting here is that images are refracted in the process as something gets lost in the translation from analog to digital. Jack uses his imagination to bridge the gaps and complete the translation. The things that do not make it across the digital/analog gap are what Lyotard (1983) refers to as the. Jack negotiates the *différend* regarding the image realm the same way one might need to fill in the gaps that occur when translating from one language to another.

While seeming unthreatened by any need to change his hands-on painting processes, Jack describes his art making practice as one that straddles digital and virtual ways of approaching image development through his computer, with the manual procedures he uses for actually applying the paint to canvas. Jack calls upon the digital self that he developed growing up looking at continuous series of fleeting images through video games which he has continued to educate himself through the use of computer imaging programs and the Web. He reworks this digital self in the service of his hands-on painter self, to retain what he calls a spontaneity, apparently unaffected by other mechanical or digital processes. This act of translating between manual and digital modes of art making is key to my investigations and is an issue that prompted my conversations with artists in the first place.

The *différend*, or that which is refracted in translation underscores my analysis of the ways artists are affected by using computers in their art making practices and highlights the tension created when they work jointly with two different forms of visual language. Developing strategies such as Jack has done is one way that Collins (1995) suggests individuals are also dealing with excess digital information. As routine aspects of daily life and work are increasingly computerized, we all must find new strategies for translating between analog and digitized procedures, information and white noise (Burbules 2000; De Lillo 1985; Fidler 1997; & Johnson 1997), and accessing different aspects of self so we may negotiate these multiple terrains (Negroponte 1995, Turkle 1995).

Jack recognizes that he is a visually oriented person because of the abundance of electronically mediated images that enveloped his childhood. He, in turn, chose to create images, but in a way that would ground him to the physical, material world and to a self that is immersed in the tactility of things made by hand, which is part of his heritage and who he is.

> I don't have deep meaning behind what I paint where I think there's more to what I'm doing than there is. Don't get me wrong, I take it very seriously . . . it's a passion, it's an obsession, but to some degree you can't take it too seriously and I paint because . . . I can't even give you an answer. It's just an inner thing that drives me to want to paint . . . I've always been very visual and coming from, I don't really want to single out my generation or anything but . . . you know you grow up watching Sesame Street where you have just like . . . boom . . . boom . . . boom . . . you know it was coming at you just quick cuts . . . very image oriented and . . . MTV and the way videos are filmed . . . it seems to be all intense and boom, boom, boom, so being a visual person, I feel compelled to create visual things because I've just sucked so much of that up . . . my processes of working, putting paint down with large trowels or mops whatever, you know it sort of gives you this image of who you are and what you do.

At the end of the interview, Jack thanked me for including him. He said that he had never really thought about the effects of digital culture on his working processes that he claims are very modernist in nature (something that he feels people expect of a much older artist). He said that the topic really interested him and he wanted to find out more about what the effects might be. He felt that the questions really made him work hard and reflect on what it is that he really does as an artist.

**Donna**

We met at Donna's home in Hamilton in the afternoon while her children were at school. Donna is a 47-year-old at-home mom as well as an artist, web designer and entrepreneur. Like Peter, Donna was also an archeologist in her academic life. She has mixed feelings about the discipline and decided to leave academic life just short of completing her doctoral thesis work. We conducted the interview in Donna's studio which is located at the back of the house just off her kitchen (a very active space in the house) with windows that look out onto the garden. Donna's studio is a small space, but well organized with different objects and bits and pieces of images and drawings/ideas carefully placed within her view. The computer is not located in the studio, but rather upstairs in her bedroom. We both sat at her work table with the tape recorder between us.

As Donna talked, she was very expressive with her hands. She would draw with her finger on the table, tracing the images or designs she was talking about. Often she mentioned "that's a good question" and at times was trying to be more analytical in her approach to the question, frequently saying "the archeologist in me . . . " Evidence of her work was all around us and most prominent was her notes, sketches, and the colour wheels she had created.

Donna was concerned that the interview questions blurred the boundaries between different computer uses, i.e., standard commercial programs, the Internet and email, and the Web. She believed they were separate entities and affected her differently (however we did not really get into the effects of the Internet other than she uses email, but does not chat or use newsgroups). She needs to compartmentalize these different functions into different spaces that can relate to each other, as well as to how she envisions their usefulness within her art making practice. For Donna, there is no room for the blurring of distinctions.

Donna, however, is emphatic about her need to work with her hands, including imposing handmade marks on top of the computer manipulations and sketches she uses as mockups for larger works on canvas. For Donna, the hand spiritually identifies her in a way that is reminiscent of D.H. Lawrence's utterings from *Why the Novel Matters* Lawrence contends that the hand "is just as much *me* as is my brain, my mind, or my soul. Why should I imagine that there is a *me* which is more *me* than my hand is?"

This relationship Donna has with her hand is similar to Claire's. They both work to retain a kind of aura, not unlike the aura that Benjamin (1968) speaks of, which is grounded in time, space and context. These are notions that are very much tied to the materiality of the physical world and notions of retaining a unique original, even though the hand may be considered to reproduce what the artist's eye perceives. However, with the introduction of electronic and digital technologies, the original becomes reproduce-able on a much grander scale. Digital technology is causing artists to rethink concepts of the original as they themselves are gaining the capabilities to appropriate, reproduce and disseminate from the similar places (the studio and the computer) where an "original" is conceived.

Donna's ideas for making art often come from the everydayness of her surroundings. She collects mental images of banal scenes and objects she sees when walking in her neighbourhood and from her own personal history. These things influence the images she produces in conjunction with her knowledge of different landscapes gained from her work as an archeologist. Like Claire, she calls on this gathering and juxtaposing of bits of information and image as a way of constructing new meaning.

Donna is also very influenced by her own dreams. They sometimes become a source of subject matter for her in the same way that Claire allows her ideas to mix and stew a bit over time. While Claire's results come out as her "cross pollinations" from her information gathering sessions, Donna's come through her dreams.

> When I'm working on art, I get into rather vivid dreaming, just before waking up and often there's some very strong visual images.

Similarly to Peter and Claire, Donna is also continuously influenced by work she has already produced in ways that enable her to see her own evolution through the images she is developing. She looks back on past work for cues to paths she might explore. In the same way that Claire says she maintains a dialogue with her work, both existing pieces and works in progress, Donna turns back on her own images and texts as a way of informing her current work. Peter also refers to past texts through his many sketch books, drawings and digitized portfolio. The three artists work with a form of intertextuality (Barthes 1977) where past and present work informs potential work that is yet to be done. Claire, Donna and Peter are all influenced by intertextuality as part of their working processes. Yet, intertextuality is not a new concept to artists since new work frequently refers back to other work the artist has done and brings with it a new reading of those older texts embedded in the new texts and images that are created. I am describing images here as interchangeable texts. However, as Claire, Peter, and Donna have discovered, interchanging digital texts with analog texts calls for some degree of translation that in itself is potentially yet another text to be considered.

Again, like Claire and Peter, Donna's way of developing her ideas and the texts I have been describing is strongly influenced by the act of writing and recording, a process closely linked with her archeologist self and a process similar to Peter's, also a former archeologist. Peter records ideas through gestures and images, Donna records feelings and reactions she is having, and Claire documents quotes, film scenes, moments in particular music and the actions of others in a way that details everyday life. All three artists' thinking and making processes are very much tied to hand marking and writing as an entry into actual art production. Donna says of her recording habits,

> I started writing down how I feel about a topic or what it says to me. I explore it that way because it is a more personal way of getting closer and closer to what appeals to me with the idea or the topic. Sometimes when I'm painting I will write about the painting itself . . . I think what happens is you react to your own work as the viewer once you've started the image. I'll try and absorb as much as I can, especially sort of synchronous things that happen when I'm thinking of a topic or idea for an image. I'll also do a lot of research and exploring. I'll do sketching, I'll do collage, I'll explore how to make the image or how to compose, how to tolerate, do the image, and occasionally I'll mock it up on Adobe Photoshop on the computer. I'll also write about it and explore my own feelings about it and I'll dream about or visualize what I want it to look like. And then I'll do a literature search if I feel that is what is required.

Donna contemplates on her own processes, again like Claire, to see what kinds of images are surfacing as a result of her researching, collecting, documenting, and dreaming. Referring to Grumet again, Donna is an active interpreter of her own journey, studying her "processes and biases of selection at work" (1981a:141).

Donna claimed that she is not just intuitive in her approaches to ideas, but needs to progress through "my nice stages and steps." In this way, she retains the delineations between different aspects of her processes unlike Claire who suggests that it is the mixing up of different processes that cause new things to surface.

Donna's stages and steps retain a structure that is superimposed over her thinking about making art and also using a computer. The different spaces and places for different aspects of everyday life are important to Donna's negotiating various terrains whether they are physical or virtual.

The Internet and particularly email has facilitated a greater sense of community with other artists for Donna. She says that she tends to contact artists whose work she has seen to discuss various aspects of their working processes.

> I will write other artists now, where I would never sit down with pen and paper and write an artist or say I liked your show before. If I have their email address, probably if I know them, I would write them about their work. And make comments and ask how they did certain things . . . I've got a stronger sense of community because I do come across people's names on the web and I'll look at art shows and art listings and I will communicate with artists through email.

However this is activity that is separate from any sense of art production. The email communications are not included in the communities that Donna walks through looking for the banal scenes and objects that are reinterpreted in her paintings. It is research and possibly some form of confirmation of belonging to a particular group of individuals that are called artists. It is a kind of confirmation that can be achieved anonymously, especially for those who are not sure about the larger art community and its effects on a fragile artist's ego. Robyn has also found anonymity a great strategy when broaching others about her work.

Donna separates her relationship to the computer into distinct categories. She has a greater sense of community through her email communication, which has a different place from the information on the Web, which is different than her relationship to digital imagery and image making. She stressed more than once that (unlike the other artists in the study) she needed to keep the separate functions compartmentalized in their uses.

> I get a little confused because there's the image making, the looking at other images, the whole realm of digital imagery and digital technologies and how that's influenced the making of images. Then there is this whole information of texts - textual information that's available on the web. I think that with the digital imagery which has been quite tremendous . . . there's a whole realm that has opened up for artists to explore and there are people who consider themselves computer-based artists who do that. And then there's the textual part of the web . . . most web sites tend to be very graphical and textual oriented and they do this thing called information overload when they put a lot of really layered information and you get this blast of information coming at you. This is not necessarily what you want to do with a work of art . . . whereas the Web is just thousands and thousands of ideas coming at you quickly.

Donna's need to delineate the different functions of the computer highlights a form of site-specificity of internal computer spaces as they relate to function. While the computer is a place in itself that is contained within another place that of the studio, or in Donna's case the bedroom, there are also different delineations in the virtual realm that can be perceived as spaces attached to particular functions whether they are for entertainment, image, sound, and text production, communication, organization or publication.

Anna McCarthy (2001) studied site specificity in relation to the placement of television sets in non-domestic spaces. Her work is useful here in determining the ways in which the computer appliance may imply particular uses in relation to its site-specificity. McCarthy suggests the site specificity of an actual media form is useful when thinking about its "social and spatial operations" (2001:2). How is the computer situated through social discourse and practice within the artists' studios in contrast with their kitchens or bedrooms? In the case of most of the artists I interviewed, their computers are situated in a place other than the studio space used for hand making art. This calls into question what power it is given as a tool for making, and then again, the ways in which its presence might disrupt the ambience of the studio space. The computer is perceived to serve the artists' local needs, which are quite distinct from the macro level connections to be made via the Internet and the Web. Recognizing that the computer assumes some sort of site-specificity, we (artists) may, as McCarthy claims, "gain a far clearer sense of the political geography" of these media forms and the ways in which "the mechanisms that connect small-screen practices to the global networks of power" are affecting the ways artists are constructing meaning within these new spatial organizations (p. 16).

How are the variable functions of the computer delineated within certain contexts, and in particular within the different perspectives, uses and resistances put forth by the artists? Donna's need to designate the different functions of the computer to different conceptual spaces contrasts with the other five artists' attitudes toward the computer as a tool of sorts. They do not emphasize or elaborate on the technical distinctions between its various uses. They treat their computers as an all-purpose tool, a kind of digital Swiss army knife that allows them to research, communicate, produce documents, try on ideas, view the work of other artists, view their own work, manipulate images, and download music. Donna's issue raises some very interesting themes that deserve greater discussion. Instead of diverting my focus at this point however, I discuss the places and spaces of the computer and theories of site-specificity at length in chapter five.

Donna's work as a Web designer has allowed her another way to experiment with her own aesthetic sensibilities, treating the screen like a canvas (Manovich 2001). She is open to how digitization can extend her imagination, facilitating new possibilities in ways traditional hand drawing and sketching may not. Image manipulation programs such as Photoshop have offered her "a way of changing and manipulating images quickly, coming up with new ideas that I wouldn't necessarily have thought of by doing sketches." The computer manipulations have even furthered the dream imagery.

> I'll start dreaming some imagery . . . and an image had appeared that required repetition so I thought the computer would be the very best place to take a shape and repeat and repeat and repeat, so I used that as the basis of the design, and in fact I did the whole graphic layout because it is easiest on the computer . . . but it was always a jumping off point. What I create there is not the art. It's a sketch of an idea not the product which to me is the physical canvas and the paint on it.

Donna does not appear to consider the computer-based sketches to be a finished art product, even though the digital printout has its own physicality. It seems to be another strategy that Donna uses to separate virtually produced images from hand produced art. However, while in most instances Donna keeps physical and virtual processes separate, even designating digital works of a lower status, she has allowed the effects of seeing her work on a pixilated screen to influence what could happen on the canvas screen. New texts are created through the virtual image to physical object translation. A dialogic relationship forms between Donna's analog and digital processes where traces of one become evident in the other affecting its appearance because of the conversation. The digital and handmade works become heteroglossic through what Bakhtin suggests is the interaction of utterances between two voices (Groden & Kreiswirth 1997). Donna is responding to the conversation in ways that make her rethink and reevaluate the relationship between digital images and her hand-produced work. This is similar, but also different, to Jack's strategy of working backwards from the digital depiction by imagining the work in the physical world as a form of translation. In Donna's case, the handmade quality of the work is refracted because of the digital translation. Both Jack's and Donna's approaches to translating between digital and handmade work acknowledge that something changes, something gets lost in translation, never to remain the same, while something else may be gained. They are both dealing with a gap that is sometimes welcome and sometimes agitating.

Donna's experience of viewing her own work on the Web influenced her direction with colour, even though she understood that what she was viewing was distorted by the inaccurate saturation of the pixilated screen colours.

> Pictures that were more neutral toned, that were softer, appealed to me much more when looking at them on the screen than the strong paintings and I tend to be a very strong coloured painter . . . But the screen echoing at you and vibrating, I thought maybe I need to tone it down. I have been approaching this change of colour, deliberately.

The computer screen reflection has added new possibilities for viewing the work just as digital manipulation programs have added new opportunities in terms of making imagery and facilitating the imagination. When asked what extends your imagination more, the computer or a sketch pad, Donna replied,

> It's an extension, but it doesn't quite have the freedom, yet it sure does tweek the imagination in its own way. I'm saying yes and no at the same time. Certainly it [the computer] extends your range of possibilities - the digital imagery, what you can do with it, the speed at which you can create . . . It's an addition, it's an expansion. It's not better or worse though.

Donna is describing the différance of including the computer within her art making practice. It both expands and limits her imagination, in Derridian fashion it can be present and absent. It "sets in play a movement of undecidability" (Collins & Mayblin, 2000, p.77). It is this state of undecidability that can provoke an uncomfortableness for Donna because her working practice appears to be so structured.

**Jin**

Jin is a 33-year-old artist, gallery owner and curator. He has been working on his own practice of art making since 1993 and has known he wanted to be an artist since he was a child. He makes contemporary drawings and paintings on MYLAR or paper, as well as some etchings. Due to his gallery and curatorial responsibilities, Jin finds time, usually once a week, to devote to art making. In spite of the time constraints, he is fairly prolific and exhibits regularly. Jin spends an average of six to ten hours per day on a computer using it for communication purposes, work related word processing, and graphic design.

The interview took place at the gallery where Jin is a co-owner and curator. He has also exhibited his work there. The gallery was closed to the general public. However, the other co-owner and a young gallery assistant were working in the background, and cataloguing works that had just arrived for the next scheduled exhibition. Music played, the phone rang, and activity continued as Jin and I sat on a couch positioned right in the middle of the gallery. We were surrounded by the current group exhibition of drawing that was curated by Jin. He defined drawing in his curatorial statement which accompanied the exhibition,

> Drawing is a form of communication or language that dates back to pre historic times. Without this form of communication modern day language would not exist. No matter what country or culture drawing plays an integral yet fundamental part in communication. Drawing is an individual expression that distinctly displays one's personal style or aesthetic. Drawing will always hold an important place within every culture due to its ability to transfer or carry a message.

Jin uses the mark-making form of drawing for his own art making practice and exhibition. His curatorial premise as quoted above is complementary to the context from which Jin was speaking during our interview. Jin's art making processes while appearing for the most part to be intuitive, a position he agrees with, are indeed influenced by the changing cultural environment he immerses himself in and a sense of global-ness that underlines his outlook on our changing times.

> I don't work like a lot of artists who do all the sketches in sketch books on a daily basis because my job is always at the gallery. I am surrounded by artwork and the artists, so it's hard for me to focus on my own art work . . . I develop my ideas in my brain while I'm sleeping and when I wake up, when I'm taking a bus, when I'm driving, or when I'm on a road trip with friends. I get a lot of ideas when I go to movies. I get inspired by everything every day, and it just develops in my brain and it just organizes in there. By the time it hits me, that's the time when I want to create a work. I usually take four months or two months off and furiously just work on it and then once my body of work is finished, I don't know what's next. I go into this black hole and I get scared with all that anxiety and then it comes back to me again, so that's where I start. It just comes natural . . . Mostly my work is based on memory and nostalgia, cultural references, colours, textures and text from different cultures, so I'm creating with identity. I am a Korean born artist that immigrated here when I was young so right now my new work is all about the Korean folk tale stories, so I try to recapture my old childhood memories that are more like the story books, bedtime stories, legends from Korea so I'm trying to capture that. Definitely there is a cultural reference in my work.

Jin suggests that these various influences are ever present in his work. Like Claire and Robyn, Jin absorbs all the details in his everyday negotiations and travels as substance for his working processes. Even though he may focus on a particular theme like the Korean folk tales, the ways in which that particular subject matter is interpreted and reconstituted as imagery is filtered through the collected bits of his own everyday-ness. Jin is apparently nondiscriminating in what counts as influencing his work.

> Everything is important to me. I am inspired by many different things. What I see in the magazines, movies, and communication all impacts on me and when I'm creating something whether consciously or unconsciously, whether I like it or not, the work comes out from that base of information so I cannot hide that from my body of work.

Jin says that he uses books and his own memory for references for his image making.

> I'd rather just spend a lot of time reading and going to see movies and talking to people and reading magazines and getting ideas - and what I really like is I cut out and collage and origami them all together, and I write notes about them and it comes together to me as one . . . I have a basis in drawing and painting, and my works on MYLAR show this, oil sticks and charcoal, all kinds of stuff. It's always been mixed media. I began to think about how far I can push this into other ways of doing work . . . I'm interested more in manipulating the media . . . into one to another. Not only that, also the trick of changing the different mediums to etching to paintings to maybe thinking about doing a video film pieces, next, or in the future.

Media manipulation has always been a way that artists have experimented with different processes and procedures that enable them to break with modernist conventions. Jin's desire to manipulate his materials so that evidence of the actual process becomes subverted is not new. Many conceptual artists have promoted the ideas behind their work in ways that undermine traditional processes, removing evidence of "the how it is made" in exchange for "what it is saying." Many artists also make crossovers between static image making and time-based media such as video. However, as Jin's conversation and creations imply, the emergence of computer use within art making practice has prompted a number of artists to rethink their approaches to mixing various media forms, and the manipulation capabilities afforded by new technologies have offered new opportunities for these interchanges.

Jin's art making practice and perception of the current place of art making is grounded in the all-inclusive field of visual culture. This perception is also very much tied to the Internet and the Web and the wealth of visual resources they make available. The push-pull relationship between art and design that interests him is not a new phenomenon, but one that is increasingly challenged. For instance, design has usually implied that functionality was a key consideration of the designer/maker. However, more recently designs for what appear to be functional objects such as Philippe Starck's juicer, do not function well at all, but are beautiful to look at. It is apparent that Starck favoured the aesthetic appearance of his product over its ability to fulfill its function. Boundaries that once distinguished high and low culture, the fine arts from popular culture and from the design industries are blurring with the advent of visual culture and one of its particular dissemination vehicles - the Web. Jin implies that design has become the *uber* category of almost all things visual that define our manufactured culture and aesthetics. This seems more apparent in the attitudes of the younger artists who grew up with a continuous onslaught of images according to Jack than it did for Claire, Peter, and Donna. Jin describes his philosophy on the presence of design within his environment,

> These days, the way that young people look at what contemporary art should be or how they'd like to approach it is very much referenced by designs. Designing is all about art, and design is a new form of art and art is an old form of design, so it's basically the same thing. How do we divide that? It's always been very blurred between the two subjects, and a lot of people like to say art is different, art shouldn't be compared with fashion, art shouldn't be compared with that. I don't think there's any more boundaries like that. I think people should be more open . . . don't be afraid of mixing them and combine everything together. I mean that's the way music has been developed over the years, fashion as well, and without those kinds of experimental ideas - it's what makes me curious . . . Design has always been a very important part of our human technologies and civilizations. It is not a surprise to see we're hooked on the Internet and E-Mails . . . we're more connected to the world faster than ever, and we're more aware of what happens on the other side of the world . . . design is a new form of art and technology can help you to make it faster and better quality with more interesting manipulations that we haven't come up with before.

Jin has a web site of his work and prefers to preview the work of gallery artists through the Internet, although he does make some distinctions in his aesthetic preferences maintaining that digital representations are not always adequate substitutes for work created by hand. He also relegates the status of digital imagery to a level that is not quite as good, as visually, and perhaps physically satisfying as images that are created by hand. He suggests that digital images are lacking in some visual and physical qualities that are inherent in the aura presented by handmade work. However, always conscious of the new global-ness offered by the Internet, and his continuous excitement at being a participant in this global-ness (a desire also shared with Robyn, and to some extent by Peter), Jin attempts to employ up to date technologies in his day to day negotiations with the world.

> My works - usually the photographs and the installations, look the best on web sites. Paintings and drawings - paintings are the hardest ones because the textures and sensitive details sometimes do not appear on jPEG. We have great technologies but they cannot be our own hand.

Jin is very interested in the merger between what his hand can do and how his actions are aided by technology. He knows there are possibilities, but he must also rethink the importance of his own handmade marks. "It always fascinates me what we do with our own vision and our own hands plus technologies." He believes very strongly that artists must be connected to the outside world and to the other side of the world so they can know what is going on around them. Greene (2000) suggests that these connections have the potential to develop an individual's wide-awakeness to the world. Jin informs himself incessantly about the world around him. He says,

> [I]t's all about getting the right combination . . . connecting with the Internet and just research, a lot about what's out there and who's doing what, and am I doing something somebody's already done, or am I making

> any points out of this body of work. Those sorts of things are important, so connecting with many sources is quite important . . . I hope it (my work) impacts on people's minds. What it would be like to live in different cultures and have different kinds of colour, different kinds of identities and issues and cultural references . . . I like to investigate different cultures and renderings between the different cultures and getting that information together and help people to understand where I'm coming from, and who I am as an artist, and not just my own culture . . . helps people to be more open-minded, to understand better each other, especially these days. We have to be tuned into our own soul and be more open-minded . . . so that's part of my process - creating my own passion to help myself to be more spiritual . . . I am still who I am, but I really don't invest that much time in doing that much work digital-wise, so I can't really say I am different or I am the same. And I think that is the question I would like to ask in the future. How will it change me? I don't know if I can answer that yet . . . I think it's important to not be afraid of investing your time into something that you have never done. My favourite line is: 'Travel somewhere that you have never been before.

Jin also appears to be grappling with the *différend* when he says "I can't really say I am different or I am the same" yet not with the same hint of agitation that Donna and Jack suggested. Jin embraces both physical and virtual worlds as important to informing both his work and his outlook on life. Even though travel is important to Jin, it need not be physical. However his work hinges on the physicality of his hand making processes and it is sensual tactility which appears to ground him to the world around him.

**Exploring the phenomena within the stories**

This chapter has been dedicated to presenting the six artists that I interviewed for the micro case studies and my analysis of their stories. Both the artists' descriptions and my analysis suggest the varied ways artists explore ideas through different technological and social contexts, and, in particular, highlight some of the similarities between their perceptions about manual methods of producing images and new opportunities that arise through the engagement of digital technologies. In some instances the artists made seemingly contradictory comments, as in the case of Claire, Jack and Donna. These tensions open up questions regarding how traditional artists recognize the ways in which they maneuver - or not, between manual and digital worlds as they investigate new ideas, concepts, and procedures.

An important aspect of studying the phenomena of how artists are integrating computers into their manual art making practices is to underline their particular ways of resisting new technology. What strategies do the artists employ for circumventing particular aspects of technological use that makes them uncomfortable or even threatens their grounded manual procedures? How are they deferring their own immersion into computer culture as it relates to their studios and how is the proximity of their computers to their manual practices a factor that influences this deferral? As well, the artists' stories suggest ways they are translating between analog and digital procedures for producing images. Often this entails negotiating and sometimes filling in gaps that are left from the translation process. These are all issues that require further attention and elaboration. The artists' descriptions hint at a myriad of questions they have about the place of computer technology within their own studio spaces and how they are grappling with both challenges and innovations that are impacting on their hand making processes and their self-making as artists.

Studying the phenomena found in these artists' experiences and perspectives have brought to light what is at stake in their becoming digital-based artists, and what is to be gained or lost by integrating manual and digital procedures in their art making practices. What tensions surface from the dialogue between the manual and digital approaches the artists are employing? These questions resurface again and again throughout the artists' conversations and my analysis and underscore the particular themes I have extracted for elaboration in chapter four.

In the next chapter, I examine the artists' stories more closely in terms of common themes and threads that are woven throughout the conversations. As the artists work through different junctures in their making, they reveal new levels of "sensitivity and integration" that might otherwise go unnoticed or unstudied (De Kerckhove 1995:135). The themes that arise as the artists recount their experiences of integrating computers into their art making touch on issues of control and of their bodies' connection to making with computers. The location of the artists' computers in relation to their art making production studios prompts questions regarding space and place, both within the computer itself, as well as outside its electronic box in relation to its placement in artists' domestic or working environments. How are these spaces embodied by the makers and their making? It is through an interrogation of these concerns and questions that the stories not told begin to emerge. Highlighting these particular issues opens up further discussion about how the artists are relating to new technologies in ways that are not so readily apparent from their own recountings and what it means to be a hand maker of art in relation to physical and virtual spaces.

# CHAPTER FOUR: THE EXPLORATION

## Selected themes embedded in the artists' conversations and the gaps in translation

Chapter three presented the artists' stories with my analysis of how they are integrating computers into their primarily handmade practices. However, further excavation into the artists' dialogue found gaps created by the translations of their storied accounts. Three particular themes emerged that prompted questions needing closer examination. Through a process of immersion and elaboration this chapter explores and elaborates on the three themes that focus on:

i) the ways in which artists research ideas for making art, in particular, changes that occur in the research process when it moves from the physical world to the virtual world on the Web.

ii) the ways in which artists' image producing capabilities have been hampered and/or extended by digital manipulation and reproduction. Issues of control arise in relation to the artists' increased control over their hand rendering abilities via computer programs versus the computer programs' control over the artists. I am specifically focusing on what is gained or lost in the transfer or translation of that perceived control.

iii) the artists' attachments and commitments to the physicality of making art by hand yet at the same time, their enticement to digital imagery and simulation. The tensions between sensual tactility and seductive visual-ness are highlighted here.

Technology is a term that is not easily defined, yet I cannot escape using the word when I am referring to actions and procedures used by artists in both manual and digital modes. Is *technology* the means to make objects, is it the procedure for making, is it a way of "bringing forth" in the Heideggarian sense that I have already mentioned, or is it one of those amorphous terms that defies singular definitions or contexts? Williams' (1988) investigation of the social and cultural practices inscribed on particular keywords describes the term technology using various references to craft, making, mechanical applications, production and construction, patterns and systems. He suggests that technology is "a system of such means" of "a particular construction or method," (p.315). We use these systems and constructions to help us interpret how we can move through the world and develop an understanding of what we see around us. The word technology is fluid. It does not relate only to objects or constructions and procedures, but also in a Foucauldian sense to practices and sets of relations that implicate structures of power. As well, technology relates to the ways in which individuals construct diverse notions of space and place, and, as Arendt (1998) alludes to, the ways in which we humans envision ourselves as driven by our needs, the greatest of which is ensuring our preservation.

Yet, as Götz suggests, there also appears to be an anxious contemporary contention that many individuals believe technology is something that must be "conquered, tamed or overcome" (2001:81). This attitude surfaces among many of the artists at various points in their conversations as they describe the need to regain control from the limitations set by digital programs and the importance of privileging their own hand markings over those made by a machine. The artists need to establish their own philosophies about technology in relation to how they integrate and exchange many different kinds of procedures and ideologies within their art practices. Götz suggests "[w]e do not need freedom from technology, but liberation from the constraint to see technology in exclusively industrial, instrumental, non-aesthetic and nonphilosophical ways" (2001:84). In the words of D.H. Lawrence in *Education of the People I,* "the machine is in us, or it would never come out of us." I use the word "technology," to describe the different systems we create for ourselves in order that we may discover, explore, reveal, disclose, and present the conjunctions and relations between our diverse experiences and interpretations of being in the world. In this way, the artists' stories presented in this research are all affected by their own technologies of self-making or autopoiēsis, by the systems of methods and constructions they have developed for exploring their experiences of being in the world and their ways of becoming as artists. These systems help them understand the poetics of their creating selves within the enframing context of our electronic and digital culture. This dialect between poiēsis and enframing is performed by Tim Griffins (1997) in an online essay about his own creative process titled Mass Production: Techne & Poesis.

As part of my own immersion into the selected themes I have appropriated and adapted Aronowitz & Menser's theory that assigns technology to specific "methodological distinctions" which may be seen at work within art making practices (1996:15). The first distinction is ontological. It describes the complexity of what *technology* is through interaction with *culture* and *science.* The work posits a way of meditating this interaction as they move through the world interpreting what they see around them. These mediations involve the artists' own beliefs, assumptions, values, and reservations about art making and being in the world. They also involve authoritative constructions of the artists' knowledge practices about what art is expected to be and how artists are presumed to create. These authorities are historical, cultural, social, economical, and political.

The second distinction, the pragmatic, is what technologies do, their social functions. In the case of the artists interviewed, it addresses the modes in which both computer-based and manual forms of technologies service their needs, efficiently, economically and creatively, extending their imaginations in new ways. Within the pragmatic space of computer technology, the artists research their ideas and find new procedures for manipulating and producing images. However, efficiency and innovation may not always take precedence over familiar ways of working. The perception that technology always provides new and improved ways of working is contestable, particularly when questions arise as to how the technologies are shaping the artists.

The third distinction is phenomenological or "how technologies affect [the artists'] experience in ways that are not bound to questions of function" (p.9). This is also the site where the translating between different technological forms takes place. Technology provokes excitement, anxiety, intrigue, and tension affecting the different ways that individuals interpret the world, and as evident by the artists' accounts, sometimes in ways that are contradictory to who they thought they were. Moreover, the phenomenon surrounding a particular technological apparatus or procedure might take precedence over the pragmatic efficiencies of a counterpart. For example, the artists privilege their laborious hand markings over the more efficient drawing procedures facilitated by computer programs. As has become evident through the artists' stories, the hand maintains a kind of aura that the computer does not.

The phenomenological distinction also involves philosophies of space and place in relation to the constructing and socializing practices of technology. How are the artists shaped by technology and how do others' assumptions (within the broader culture) about technology affect their own socializing and working practices? The artists' stories are affected by these three methodological distinctions of technology at different points in the conversations. They not only illuminate the themes I have extracted in terms of a theoretical position, but also demonstrate the complexity of the term *technology* in relation to a wide range of practices across both physical and virtual world contexts.

## Connecting the themes to the larger question of how artists are using computers

I would like to return to the original impetus for this inquiry, the question of how artists are using their personal computers to assist or replace their hand making procedures, and the issue of how this affects how they see themselves as makers of art work. These two questions are important to refer back to when considering the various themes that emerge from the artists' descriptions of their engagements with computers. These themes are also composed of sub-themes and issues that illuminate the complexity of the artists' endeavours to re-position themselves as creators in an environment that is increasingly influenced by digital forms of image production, manipulation and expression.

The first prominent theme is the pervasive practice of researching ideas and subject matter for producing images and creating work. All of the artists at one time have looked to resources on the Web during the preliminary research stages of developing new work. They view the Web as a large electronic library, however useful or cumbersome it can be. The artists described the ways in which they have been rethinking their past relationships to libraries, and, in turn, have reconfigured their approaches to research using the electronic resources of the Web. They describe how they straddle the convenient access to abundant information on the Web and the grounded feeling of the concrete materiality of books and other printed material, as well as the social aspect of researching in a public library. Through these discussions, most of the artists describe how they have exchanged the comfort of the crafted materiality of library books, with the efficiency of researching through a computer screen in cyberspace.

The key issue of how artists are researching their ideas on the Web involves several sub-themes that relate to the depth of research that can be achieved, how excessive amounts of information can lead to different states of aporia which I define as an impasse or insurmountable point (*c.f.* Burbules 2001), as well as a discussion of whether one researches a subject or topic on the Web as opposed to researching abstract ideas which are not yet narrowed down into subjective categories. In this case, some of the artists distinguished between the ability to research only subjects, not ideas which they suggested were a limitation. I challenge this concept to some degree as subjects cannot be divorced from ideas altogether. One can have an idea that they begin to flesh out across multiple subjects. All the artists agreed however, that the Web allows them to find information they need and "bring it home" in ways that are more efficient, and in some cases more connective than what they have experienced before (De Kerckhove 1997:132).

A second prominent theme arising from the interviews is how computers and digital imaging have facilitated opportunities for the artists to *manipulate* and *reproduce* imagery, extending their pragmatic technical abilities, their imaginations, and the possibilities for creating new work or re-viewing existing work in new forms. This issue again arises as a multi-sided debate. Various sub-themes emerged as the artists were intrigued, fascinated, and mesmerized with new found possibilities. Although, at the same time, they were conscious of the program designer or web designer as an authoritative figure or electronically mediated Other who retained some element of control over the manipulation process.

The issue of control is very much tied to the production of imagery in several ways. The artists' gained control over the presentation and production options and values available through computer programs and digital manipulation. They were able to develop images in new ways that did not depend on high degrees of hand-rendering skills. However, there is the issue of the external control imposed by program designers through the scope and limitations embedded in the programs the artists used. At times the artists described how they gained the freedom and mobility to explore and create, while at the same time how they were conscious of the program as a form of a collaborator in that process, leaving them without full autonomy and somewhat under the control of a master program authority.

A third key theme, and the most prominent one among the six artists, is that of the contest they experience between the seductive authority of digital technologies such as the Web and digital imaging programs on the one hand, and a yearning for the physicality of the material art object along with their immersion in its handmade production on the other. Four of the six artists, Peter, Donna, Claire and Jack, described the various ways they felt almost divided or split, in their relationship to the possibilities offered by their home computers as an aid for their making processes. The other two artists, Jin and Robyn, both young and emerging, did not describe their relationship to the technology as uncomfortable in any way, just a necessary part of being an artist in these times. It is this theme that stimulates thinking about technology beyond mere function and invites a theoretical deconstruction of various phenomenological factors that influence the ways in which artists are using computer and manual procedures together.

## Research in relation to art and image production

Researching ideas through both image and text-based sources is a key practice that initiates the artists' beginning of a new body of work. This practice becomes interwoven with the making as the artists move through the developmental processes of their art production. The artists' ways of researching are varied and include many sources including their own reflections and commentary about their work. The artists talked about writing and language as an integral part of their research and creative processes. They made connections to their work by writing some kind of text before, during and/or after their making process. Jin's work, for instance, begins with language,

> My work has always been a combination of both words, text mixture with colour patterns and some kind of shapes or forms between abstract and

> reality and so sometimes it comes to me first with a text and I get an idea that I come up with the colours and how I should render it. So I guess yes I use the text first in my mind ahead of it then it comes together naturally.

Comprehensive research contributes to the text/image exchange, and researching electronically performs an important role in Jin's ability to access a wide range of information about the different cultures and identities that inform his work. A large part of the research is done efficiently using the Web. Furthermore, Jin and many of the others are tied to language as a way of researching their ideas before coming to the images they create, and, through their own writing, they can detect in text what they were proposing to present in images.

Even Jack, who claims he does not engage in a lot of research, remarked that writing about what he was doing was increasingly important to his creative process, mostly due to his experiences at art college.

> I've taken to writing more about what I'm painting because when I went to school as a commercial illustrator, we didn't really have the opportunities to write a critique about what was happening or be able to write about theories behind what we were creating.

Jack's text and image-based research is reconstructed through the process of revisiting his work through his own writing. This process is intertwined with the performance inherent in the making that eventually leads to a work that becomes public with the potential to provoke other reconstructions of meaning. Heidegger suggests that the artists' act of making creates the base for something else to happen. He claims that "the work makes public something other than itself; it manifests something other; it is an allegory . . . something other is brought together with the thing that is made' (1971:19). Robyn relates image, language and idea very closely. Her approach to the image comes through reading the work of others in an effort to intertextualize the idea through word and image.

> I think that you can't have an image without ideas. I think that images don't stand by themselves as just image, there's language behind the image really there's ideas behind the images. I think a lot of times and this might come from magazine reading, as I look before I read. It's not that I don't think that they are interconnected or that images stand on their own as just visual stuff . . . if I'm looking at something I decide what it's about, but by reading something, someone's telling me what it's about.

The artists' varied ways of researching ideas also enable "something else" to influence them before, during, and often after making the work. The researching is a way of coming to the making by reinterpreting the narrative created by the information gleaned through a series of searches. The end work is about the art object, but it is also about the search and the new meaning the search has generated.

**The electronic library as "a fast immediate place"**

As I have already mentioned, the artists talked about researching as a way of coming to image making. Many of the artists saw the researching procedures that used the Internet and the Web as analogous in approach to researching in the public library. The artists' stories describe the electronic library of the Web as not only text based, but as image based, with the addition of sound and movement. Yet there was some debate as to whether one researches subjects or ideas on the Web. This debate played out in a few conversations.

The artists most concerned with this issue, Peter, Donna, and Claire, implied that they cannot use or type *an idea* into the keyword search outlets on the Web. They maintain that they must already be able to categorize the idea into subject or topic classifications in order to research on the Web. This is a pragmatic function that does not consider the exchange and interchange of words used in the searches that are generated by the idea. The subjects and topics are not divorced from this process or the idea that initiated the search. More pragmatically however, all the artists agreed that accessing information on the Web is much more efficient for their researching needs and it opens them up to more information, imagery, and global connectivity than the social practice of researching via books in the public library.

Peter for example has changed his practice of visiting the local library because of his access to information through the Internet and the Web.

> In terms of how I go about accessing and using information, I think it allows me to do what I want to do if and when and how I want to do it, which is something very special. For example, I go less and less frequently to public libraries. I believe very much in libraries, I think the public library system we have in Canada is unbelievable. I used it a lot in my youth, and I used it a lot in my formative education. I use it increasingly less now because I can access so much via the Web. So that's been a change.

The public library is a social, community place which enables the artist to carry out an aspect of their making in a potentially interactive way, commingling with others. Peter believes there is something lost from not actually researching in public as he used to at the public library

> Interestingly enough, there's a social aspect to libraries to research that is no longer. It's something that lacks in computer research, something that perhaps I regret because I can think of several times when researching with the presence of others it actually changed dramatically, the way it went about tackling something - that is less and less frequent because my researching is done individually, personally and usually there's no one else involved. That cuts me off from a certain kind of interaction that I actually benefit from amazingly certain particular times of my life. So that's an interesting change.

What appears to be missing for Peter is the performative act of going to a physical place that is designated as a researching space where he is seen by others who are also researching. As much as Peter's large scale drawings require a physical performance for their making through the physical stretching of his body to make the graphite marks, going to the public library involved putting his body into a "real" space where he would interact with other bodies, if only by moving through book stacks. The act of researching in the public library becomes part of the physical procedure employed for making. Being seen by others while in the act of researching reconfigures the process as a kind of performance where the artist, Peter, acts as an on-site gatherer and researcher.

Yet, Peter's decision to move to the electronic resources of the Web does not extinguish the performative act of his researching. Rather, it changes the form of the performance. The living community that is present within the public library, a group of people who witness the work of others by their simultaneous presence within the same space, is exchanged for an unseen collective audience in cyberspace. Lévy claims that "the growth of cyberspace corresponds to a desire for reciprocal communication and collective intelligence" suggesting that cyberspace "attempts to build a particular type of relationship among people" (2001:104). Just as the public library invokes social relations among people engaged in a quest for knowledge, cyberspace affects relations between individuals who can both present and request information leading to new knowledge acquisition. The performance takes on a reciprocity that reconfigures autonomous researchers into members of information gathering troupes.

As well, in cyberspace, the researchers gain the potential to be disseminators and presenters of information, interacting with like-minded people in their quest for knowledge. These new ways of acting and being in cyberspace are similar to the ways many artists have already performed the role of cyborg as "a means through which to construct new ideas, images and myths about ourselves living in a technological world" (Garoian & Gaudelius 2001:337). New media artist Laurie Anderson has strapped computers to her body and altered her speech patterns through electronic instruments as part of her staged performances. She does not become a computer, but intertwines herself with a computer which animates its presence on stage. As Lévy suggests, "the virtual doesn't replace the real; it simply increases the opportunities to actualize it" (2001:70). Through new strategies for interacting, artists are developing ways to perform across various social contexts which are both physical and virtual.

Robyn, like Peter, also described the physical differences she felt between the public library and the electronic library, however, Robyn focuses on certain procedures that she uses that have grounding in conventional practices she learned growing up. She compared the electronic framework for finding information on the Web with her memories of using the Dewey decimal system in pre-computerized libraries.

> When I was a child and we'd go to the library, you had to go through those little cards looking for something and I think maybe you needed to know what you were looking for and you needed to be a bit more defined. You needed to know a word because you had to sift through so much stuff to get what you needed. I didn't use the Internet in high school, I would have used the drawer with the cards in it at the library . . . it's so old school now. I think maybe then it wasn't such a free-for-all. Now you can type something (a word or phrase on the search engine) and you can get stuff from all over the world, anything related to that topic would just come up on the Internet. You could be rooted to anything related to that word or that sequence of words that you type in. I don't think you would have been opened up to so many things before. When I do research, and I use the Web when I'm doing research, you get all kinds of crazy stuff. You might be guided toward some kind of science periodical or something that might not be art related. I think the opportunity for finding information is greater now that we have the Internet, even though there's a lot more information you have to weed through, but sometimes it's really interesting.

Robyn confirms the potentiality of Lévy's conceptions of collective imagination and the production of information that has increased due to the interconnectivity of many individual interests. The production and presentation of information is a collaborative project that far exceeds a static collection of books and periodicals that exist in the "real" places of public libraries. The rhyzomatic network of the Web also allows for a multiplicity of thoughts, ideas and meanings to be manifested by single words, even though this is challenging for those who are hunting for specifics rather than gathering broad concepts on a subject (2001:67).

Like Peter and Robyn, Donna's sources for gathering information have also changed as she moves from a concrete library institution to the electronic libraries on the Web. With young children at home, Donna places efficiency as a priority for doing both text and image background research for her own art making. Her computer is located in the bedroom of her home and gives her much greater access to information than the public library. When I asked Donna how she approaches the preliminary research stage of her process she replied,

> It seems to me that there are two things to do. I divide the process into image research and topic research, like a literature review, a textual search as opposed to an image search. So if I'm working with an image or I want to make an image, I'll research, by looking at other artists' works that handle that kind of image or look for similar images to the one I want to make in art books and articles. The other part would be the literature search of the topic itself.

Donna's academic training and her forms of excavating for information are carried over into her research procedures that prepare her for creating work. Donna is a hunter in the way that she looks for specific information, as opposed to a gatherer, who is willing to veer off the path with the chance of finding something new (Lévy 2001:67). Donna is open to Web exploration in the name of research and looks at her web-based process in light of a virtual library experience.

> I will use the web as my own personal library available to me in my own bedroom (where her computer is located)... I'll use it for research, for looking up my medical things. It's really a form of a literary search at home rather than go to the library and go through the card catalogues or

> their digital catalogue, I'll go through their catalogue here. I'll look up web sites of interest, it expands my researching abilities, it enables me to do it more quickly or to find book titles more quickly.

Donna is not interdisciplinary in her approach like many of the others (Claire, Robyn and Jin) and does not look to cross over into other areas of study unless she develops boundaries between the parcels of information. Although she is accessing information differently and certainly more efficiently on the Web, Donna still performs her web researching through her own imagining of how she physically locates books in the categorized spaces of the public library.

> I think that if you've gone on the web, you have a question you want answered, or at least that's how I do it. So I will look for the answers and they will sometimes take you to unusual places and unusual personal experiences of individual people. I don't go to chat rooms, but I will read or find out about bulletins, and email back and forth for information . . . I don't know how deeply you can explore an idea on the web though. There tends to be a superficial quality to the information . . . I will use the web to do a literature search in my home and I can go through the library catalogue and look for articles that have been written . . . I haven't been down to the main (public) library in years looking at the art shelf, but I will research a topic on the web. It's a fast immediate place to do it. I see the web as a form of looking in the library and pulling down books and looking through them and sticking them back on the shelf and saying "yes maybe I'll take these three out and explore further.

Researching on the Web is not just about accessibility to abundant amounts of information as opposed to delving into static forms of information in library books. As a result of being connected to a larger network of individuals and information, there are implications to reconfiguring the kinds of spaces that this researching occurs within. The space of the Web allows for one's extension into a collective imagination that is far-reaching in scope, but limiting in terms of physical interaction. In contrast, the "real" place of the public library allows social interaction on a limited scale, but there is a physicality to this real space that is only imagined on the Web.

Unlike Peter and Donna, Jin describes his way of researching on the Web as a form of geographic travelling that enables him to present possibilities of the future through his work.

> We're all connected, we can travel faster than ever, we know what's going on in Europe, Asia at the same time . . . in my opinion, I feel that as an artist we're sort of living in a revolutionary century right now where we are about to change to something completely different - more futuristic, more graphic and more computer generated.

Jin contends that it is important to connect to the world and that means being connected to digital media and the Internet as a tool for looking and researching and as a vehicle for travelling throughout the world.

> I think travelling is very similar to the Internet in that the Internet is very much like travelling. It's like a time machine - you can go into the past, you can go to different counties. You can find out so many things like you can go to so many places. It's a timeless time travelling machine for me. I treat the Internet like I'm travelling to another country. It's not quite the same, but at least we can do it through these technologies. You can find yourself different information methods, sources that will help your understanding and educate yourself in different things that you've never discovered before. I think it's important to investigate them.

Jin's perspective of research and cultural production is very much affected by current theories of globalization that promote a form of time-space compression that enables individuals to become products of a multiplicity of cultural influences and ongoing social interrelations all at once (Casey 1996; Tomlinson 1999). However Massey criticizes the tendency to oversimplify theories of time-space compression suggesting that we must move beyond issues of accelerated time in relation to changing patterns of capital development and globalization by understanding that the global is implicated in local cultural production "in the very process of the formation of the local" (1994:120). Jin and the others have been influenced by their interrelations with other cultural producers on a number of levels before, but the time-space compression experienced through the Internet is a reorganization of these relations providing a heightened awareness of the implications of the global within the local. It could be said that Jin is living in the "glocal" where he negotiates both *the local* and *the global* simultaneously by experiencing them not as polarities, but as interdependent principles (Tomlinson 1999:195-196).

The place of the local is dynamic and ever-changing. Probyn distinguishes the place of the local as "locale," or "the setting of a particular event" (1990:178). These settings are more like intersections of social relations (Massey 1994) that are recognized as events that are both globally influenced as well as locally situated. The artists are impacted by new informational technologies brought to them through these events by computers. They relate to the events in new informational spaces that are accessed not only through language and image, but also through an embodied experience of the information space as both global and local. This, in turn, impacts on the artists' approaches to researching and creating meaning in their work through image and text, and their feeling of connectedness to places beyond the locales of their studios. Massey (1994) suggests that some of the relations to place will be "contained within the place; others will stretch beyond it, tying any particular locality into wider relations and processes in which other places are implicated too" (p.120). The artists are no longer autonomous creators working in a fixed space, but rather, part of a larger project of social interrelations that extend beyond their making places, affecting how they see their art practice in both local and global contexts.

**The reconfigurations of *subject* and *idea* in online research**

Several of the artists made a clear distinction between researching *subjects* and researching *ideas* online. Their main concern was whether one researches a subject or topic on the Web as opposed to researching abstract ideas which are not yet narrowed down into subjective categories. They claimed that ideas are too abstract to pinpoint down to a few keywords to be used with a web-based search engine, but subjects provoke a plethora of information, sometimes in ways that suggest unconventional linkages. Yet, *subjects* are encoded with past ideas. Robyn states that,

> The probing of an idea is trickier. I think that it is similar to [researching] subject matter because I know for me that when I have an idea about something it's always first related to images and not necessarily the language that comes from the subject matter. I don't know if I necessarily use the Web to explore an idea. I don't think I go online thinking okay I've got this idea and I try and figure it out. I think that I use the Web to find images, colour, language, and I don't think I use it like I would use a book.

Robyn however overlooks the process involved in her researching that is much more complicated than typing a keyword into the Web search engine. Seeking information whether text or image based under different subject headings is part of the process of exploring ideas and the two are interdependent.

Claire also delineates the concept of researching subjects as opposed to researching ideas on the Web.

> I think I always start with a subject and I think that ideas come in later. I don't think the Internet and the Web is very good in my opinion about nebulous things about things in the ethers. I think it is very good at concrete things, but it's lousy at communicating. It's great about information and information is about subject to me. Ideas are about many things impinging on each other at once. I cannot go and look up all the wonderful messy things, all the abstract, insubstantial, in the ether kind of stuff that comes out of human interactions. I think researching that messy wonderful stuff is not so easy on the Internet. Well, the word digital . . . cutting things up into little pieces, that's what the Internet is all about. It's not about ideas to me . . . You can give impetus or you can give hooks or you can give hints about ideas but I don't think you can really do ideas.

Claire suggests that the way of seeking information on the Web is through a series of signifiers that will lead her to specific classifications regarding particular topics. She also implies that her ideas are more like propositions or proposals that are not easily broken down by individual signifiers. For Claire, proposals are more tentative and not as easily narrowed down to a few key words for a Web search.

Both Robyn and Claire explore subjects on the Web through "links of association" (Johnson 1997). Johnson contends that the "link is the first significant new form of punctuation to emerge in centuries," (p.110). Linking is a way of making connections and relationships between things and "plays the defining role, for all the chief practical, cultural, and educational characteristics of this medium" (Landow 2000:154). The link "brings multifarious elements together in some kind of orderly unit," (Johnson 1997:111). Landow suggests that the Web promotes a way of thinking "in terms of connections" (2000:159). Landow's point is particularly useful in understanding the way in which Claire is interested in finding the intersections between various subject references she discovers through her Web searches. While many individuals may not believe they can research ideas on the Web, their act of making connections and developing associations between links to different subject areas has the potential to spark new ideas about the world and how they inform themselves about it. Even Robyn's act of linking between images can cause new relationships to emerge, thereby sparking new imaginings or ideas as she would term them. Perhaps the artists are having some difficulty with the notion of researching ideas on the Web because ideas could be considered a commingling of *subject* and *imagination.* The artists can use static keywords to delineate subjects, but imagination is more a fluid process that is not easily contained. Maintaining a clear distinction between subject and idea however is problematic due to the interdependency I have already mentioned.

Through linking and connecting, Claire uses the Web as a crucial resource for accessing the information that will move her toward ideas.

> It's a really good tool for gathering the kind of information that I need to push into my head in order for that to incubate around and influence one another. There's lots of good cross pollination. The other way that it's influenced me is the way that I have to learn not to let that information overwhelm me and get me stuck in circular thinking because I want more information because the work is going to be that much better, and then it actually keeps me from making the work.

Claire's approach to gathering information online empowers her access to what Lévy describes as a collective intelligence that combines "the experience, imagination, and spiritual energy of those who are connected to it" (2001:111). Similarly, De Kerckhove describes this empowerment as a way that can "connect living minds at work in all manner of purposeful configuration" (1997:153). While the Web is perceived to be statically presenting subject matter, it does so in an interconnected environment of human intelligence with a collective imagination that offers a multitude of ideas. Therefore, *subjects* on the Web cannot be severed from this connected community and the ideas that are generated by this community in relation to the subjects. Although, the ways in which Claire, Robyn, or any of the artists process the information about diverse subjects that are collected is indeed personal, driven by their own constructed beliefs giving way to their own imaginations and ideas. We are reminded that the ways that individuals construct their own beliefs are inherently affected by social processes.

The electronic research library of the Web is not just a framework of subjects, but rather a collective story about various individuals' interests about subjects that involve ideas, beliefs and assumptions. Furthermore, hyperlinks provide vehicles for discovering new relationships between subjects. These links are not just the connectors between various subjects, rather, as Burbules (2000) contends, they "represent a way of associating elements that inevitably affects how one understands them," and in turn, generates new ideas (p.172).

**Aporias created by excess information**

Although the Web has proven to be an abundant source of information that can be accessed conveniently, excessive information can also be problematic and sometimes physically discomforting. Efficiency of attaining needed information can be compromised by the excess of information on the Web which, in turn, presents a distraction. This leads to a state of aporia. One form of aporia is the point at which an individual recognizes that there are too many paths to choose from. Another form is when one does not recognize which path they should take (Burbules 2000:179). New pathways are developed by building bridges and means of connection that exist in the familiar. I am considering both forms as consecutive parts of the artists' ways of exploring, researching, and art making. An individual may reach what they feel is an impassable point, yet once they start to look for familiar reference points they can find clues of how to move on. Claire, finds her way by "recognizing enough familiar points of reference to reconstruct a meaningful pattern out of what is unfamiliar or foreign" (p.176).

Burbules contends that "[r]ecognition is both a discovery *and* a creation" (2000:176). The recognition of new meaningful patterns creates the foundation for further explorations by integrating the subtle variations and changes observed into what already exists. Bridges develop between the new patterns and older existing patterns as a way of integrating new information and innovations into our daily routines and practices. However, beyond gaining recognition for finding one's way, Claire also experiences what Burbules terms a "crisis of choice...when I have too many choices, or no choices, I don't have a choice; I'm stuck" (Burbules, 2000:173). Claire describes her aporic experience when she is researching particular subjects in the development of a new body of work.

> I think it [the Web] has broadened my research exponentially and it's made the crossovers hugely more interesting and hugely easier because I have access to so much more stuff. The down side of this for me, is I can overload myself with that part of the art making process so I'll get out

> there and say this is so interesting did I get everything? Did I get everything I possibly could to really influence this work properly? You have to learn when you have this love of research, and this love of information and this incredible love of ideas, that you have to find a way to temper that and say it's time to start working because you can get so in love with all this information that it either keeps you away from your work because you spend so much time researching, or you end up in a position that I sometimes end up in, where I get so overloaded that I don't begin to apply it because it's so big, it's so much.

The state of aporia is not just a psychological condition, but a physical/bodily experience as well (p.184). Anyone who has lost their way navigating the Web, confused at how they ended up where they did, will understand the physical disorientation, sometimes even discomfort that is felt. Similarly, the amount of information that an individual is faced with may render them almost paralyzed. Burbules explains that this experience is manifested on different levels, often provoking physical, feelings of discomfort. Claire experiences these discomforts during episodes of aporia. However, it is through this process of determining how to go on, choosing which way is next, that Claire can open up new possibilities for learning about her working processes and develop what Collins (1995) suggests: strategies for selecting and absorbing information in an effort to move forward.

Jack also finds the excess of information distracting at times. Although unlike Claire, he claims that his research "is probably pretty limited" when developing his ideas for painting and there is not such a strong experience of researching that moments of aporia inhibit his abilities to proceed with his work. He does not refer to the Web as a library; in fact he is the only one of the six artists interviewed that did not connect researching on the Web to researching in a library except for his mention of the Web as an *image bank* and how he used to have to go to the picture files at the Toronto reference library for his source material. Yet, the procedures he describes for attaining information on the Web are very similar to the behaviour described through the stories of the other artists.

Jack uses the Web as a convenient image bank or an archive, similar to the picture files of the Toronto Reference library. Jack contends however, that seeking images as resource material on the Web has its disadvantages, again because of excessive amounts of information that sometimes pose a distraction to getting on with his art making.

For Jack, the Web is often overwhelming.

> Access [to information] through the Internet and computers can be extremely overwhelming in that it's unlimited . . . I think I start off with good intentions, like I might sit down with an idea in mind, but for me it's often like walking into a music store. When you are on your way there, you know what to get . . . the minute you walk in the door you draw a blank and you end up walking out with 10 of something else . . . there are so many things that you can access and it can become extremely distracting.

Jack's experiences of aporia which take him away from his predetermined path is unlike Claire's in that he does not experience a physical discomfort created by a "crisis of choice," but rather a feeling of aggravation for having wasted time. Jack states that the overwhelming power of the unlimited access to information on the Web is usually connected to time constraints and deadlines. His veering off of the path is not for new discovery, but becomes impairment to finding the information he needs efficiently. Jack is not looking for interesting crossovers or diversions like some of the other artists, rather he needs particular images and information as resource material for his painting. However, when Jack does venture into cyberspace, he sees the Web as a useful resource for referencing colour combinations for his paintings.

Jin's experiences of getting lost on the Web begin with a kind of wandering off the path similar to Jack's, but he echoes Claire' claims about the enormous potential of researching on the Web. He experiences getting lost in that research as an embodied feeling, much like Claire's. As a younger artist however, he welcomes the distractions, the discomforts, and the excess. Sometimes while researching one particular topic he gets derailed onto something else which leads him on an unexpected journey he seems to relish. Jin's researching is very specific at the outset, but he is flexible and open to discovering new pathways through the electronic links to other web sources. Burbules reminds us that "there is no way to remain open to the possibility of happening upon something new if one is not prepared to accept getting lost" (2000:181). Jin takes up the challenge of forging paths that do not yet exist.

> Usually I'm very specific about subject matter for my new body of work, so I always know exactly where I'm going. I look into one [web site] and then sometimes they give you links and these links can take you to far away places, and really sometimes these links can give you more information than what you are really looking for or even really thought of. Now, I know I was only thinking of A and B and now I'm thinking of K and J. It's quite interesting of where that can lead you to. I always know ahead of time of what I'm going to look for, but at the same time, 'it's kind of nice to get lost and lost in space' and just wander around and see what comes out of it. It's very exponential that way . . . any artist should be open-minded and explore it [the Web] and experiment because if you don't have an open mind, you're not going to explore anything and your work will stay the same and your mentality is not going to change anything so what's the point of creating a work. You have to be tuned into the work. You have to know what's going on around. As an artist these days you have to be slightly political. You can't just say I'm not political and that is making a statement anyway. We have a future war coming up, this year, we have all kinds of stuff coming and how do we talk about those things in art? So it's important to study [research] all this and be aware of it.

Burbules offers two ways out of the doubt that is experienced through aporia which Jin's and Claire's experiences illustrate. While Claire moves toward fixed answers that will help her fulfil her responsibility to the subject she is researching, relying on connections to move her through "all that information,"

Jin experiences the aporic condition like a trailblazer even though he does look for particular ways of making "political statements." He does not necessarily need the familiarity of connective bridges. He is prepared to find his way by moving toward the unknown. Jin's description also points to a kind of aporic condition if I use definitions that describe it as a gap or void. Jin talks of getting lost yet at the same time of knowing where he is heading and being open-minded, yet tuned in. These create gaps in his text where we as readers are not quite sure of the direction he is taking us. Perhaps this is also a condition of Jin's being "glocal" and living and negotiating both local and global situations simultaneously.

**Computerized production as both taking control and being controlled**

At times the artists describe how they gained freedom and mobility to explore and create, while at the same time they were conscious of the computer program as a collaborator in that process, leaving them without full autonomy. Claire articulated the sense of another authority that she felt when using her computer, like "enter[ing] an intellectually created space made by someone else. There's a kind of something else having power over you." In the same vein, Donna has "a sensation that you're not the only person in the room . . . there's the layer in between you and what you're producing which are the computer guys who created the programs." While still cautious in her use of image manipulation programs, Donna explains that these new forms of exploring images stretch her imagination in ways that further enhance or even change the meaning she constructs in her work.

Peter suggests that many traditional artists are reluctant to collaborate in the making of images and art works. This may account for some of the resistance these artists have in using existing computer programs that are template based. He states, "a lot of artists I think are very uncomfortable with the collaborative process because they are afraid of losing self."

What is at stake for the autonomous artist who collaborates with an electronic *Other* to create work? Many writers such as De Kerckhove (1997) and Lévy (2001) believe that the collective imagination will enable all of us to more fully inhabit the world. However, these forms of collaboration are not comfortably taken up by all artists even though they are, as Peter says, "stimulated" by the control they can gain from digital image manipulation, and the quality of production that a computer facilitates. The artists' descriptions of how they used computer programs suggest a distinction between different aspects of control. Firstly, computer-assisted image production appeared to fall within two particular types of relations. They described how they gained control over the production values they could achieve by computer rather than by hand. Secondly, they perceived a level of control imposed by the authority of the computer program designers in the allowances and limitations set up in any particular program they used.

Cyberspace and the Web were also described as other computer spaces where concerns about control surfaced. Claire is quite cautious in the way she moves through cyberspace. She is wary of being tricked or seduced into informational spaces that will offend her. "There are some things that I try hard not to subject myself to because I don't want that to enter into my realm of thought processes." On occasion, she feels that her web surfing is like walking down a dark alley where you can't see the dangers. She claims,

> You have to pay more attention when you're in there [cyberspace] because there are pitfalls, there are places that are not good for you to be. It's almost like being in a dark alley at night. . . when I was learning to find good web sites and stuff, it was almost like having been abused or gone to a movie that was violent in a way that I hadn't been forewarned. And you know sometimes how you come out and you say, I've been a little bit misused by this situation.

Most of the time Claire overcomes this hesitation by using the recommendations or links provided by others when she is surfing the Web. This provides her with a more secure feeling about the spaces she enters until she reaches the point at which she is ready to take some risks. Comfort comes with the ability to recognize familiar patterns and connections that will lead her down a path toward the information she is looking for. "It's usually by some kind of recommendation that I start, I usually ride on the coat tails of somebody who I think has done some research already."

Tuan suggests that as we move between places and spaces we exchange our positions of shelter and venture (2000:54). As well, Deleuze plays out this movement in his essay "Music and Ritournello" where he describes three aspects of ritournello (1993:202). Deleuze speaks of three phases that start with the individual experiencing a displacement that leads to discomfort. This, in turn, provokes the individual to establish a centre within what she is experiencing as a degree of chaos. This centred point is home, providing a comfortable shelter. However, Deleuze claims that "home does not preexist: it was necessary to draw a circle around that uncertain and fragile center, to organize a limited space" keeping the forces of chaos outside this space as much as possible (p. 201). The third phase comes as "one opens the circle a crack . . . not on the side where the old forces of chaos press against it but in another region, one created by the circle itself. As though the circle tended on its own to open onto a future, as a function of the working force it shelters" (p. 202). These three aspects, Deleuze says, happen not successively, but simultaneously or mixed together.

In Claire's case, she begins from the shelter of web spaces that have been sanctioned by other authorities, spaces she has drawn a circle around, whether they are familiar to her as individuals or institutions she trusts. She then moves toward venturing out of those sheltered spaces to other regions which can both fascinate and intimidate, or scare her at the same time. The issue that Claire is addressing is one of authority when using computer programs or moving through cyberspace. How much authority does she comfortably entrust to the computer "other" in her quest to learn more and create more, extending herself in unfamiliar ways? Claire appears to be practising a *ritornello* as she moves across cyberspace between points of shelter and outward openings.

Lankshear and Knoeble (2000) acknowledge that digitization has impacted on many everyday social practices. They suggest adopting a new digital epistemology, a way of looking at how we acquire knowledge through computerized sources which enable individuals, in this case artists, to understand how they are managing these technologies in ways that produce meaning from their interactions with machines. Lankshear and Knoeble employ Castells' (1996) work on informationalism as a way of developing their digital epistemology. In particular, Castells' stages of telecommunications and technology development are useful for exploring how the artists in this study are in the process of coming to an understanding of the role of computer technology within their manual art production. The different stages of "automation of tasks, experimentation of uses, and reconfiguration of applications" (Lankshear & Knoeble 2000:11) move the artist's development from a practice of learning about the technology by using it, all the while staying within the constraints and limitations of the conventional presentation of the computer program, to a position of "learn[ing] by doing, thereby modifying the applications of the technology" (Castells 1996:37) and thus developing innovative uses.

To really integrate these new technologies with existing practices, "is not only to know them as a tool to be applied, but also as processes to be developed" (Lankshear & Knoeble 2000:12). The artists have the opportunity to develop their own procedures beyond the constraints of the electronic Other, in part by reconsidering what it means to make work using electronic extensions in ways that reconfigure their own conventional practices. As a result, they develop their own forms of digital epistemology through the production of a "knowledge of innovation" predicated on rule bending and breaking (Lankshear & Knoeble 2000:13). These possibilities fuel the quest to move beyond the production of objects toward the production of knowledge in ways that empower the artists to collaborate with technology rather than being controlled by it. If the artists were to consider their paints, paintbrushes and graphite as technologies, they would understand how they have already been collaborating with these processes and product makers. Working with digital technologies requires a remapping of these existing collaborations to include new relationships that are forming across more dynamic spaces.

**Drawing with a different pencil: Cyborg production and presentation**

Far greater than their concerns of control, the artists all agreed that computers have advantageously changed the ways in which they can extend their imaginations and their technical abilities when making art. Like the changes that occurred in many other areas of manufacturing, computerization of the rendering and technical manifestations of imagery have been simplified and economized through standard programs. As Donna says, it's like "drawing with a different pencil."

Peter states that computer processes allow him a level of control over the production values of his work through an elevated level of craftsmanship and skill that result in clean lines, consistent shading, and the ability to duplicate and reproduce his images without variation.

> For me a computer is not gaming, it's not; it's the excitement about being able to create something. Even when I do a letter and it's totally different. It's because it offers me a certain kind of control and quality and presentation and again I think that's something about my artist background, I'm able to control the way I put something down on a piece of paper and more so than I can do with my hand, and the problem of the handwriting being illegible is no longer a consideration if there's a mistake I can correct that. So it's how I want to get this idea out and that really stimulates me.

Peter really likes the ways in which his drawings are reinterpreted on the computer screen. The process of re-viewing his body of work in digital form provides him with a new perspective of the imagery and how it might be viewed by others through different media forms. In Peter's case, moving the very large scale graphite drawings on paper to pixilated images contained within the frame of a computer screen, offers a different reading of the images through formal properties such as scale, and opacity of the colour presented through a medium other than graphite and paper.

> For me the computer screen is very seductive, it is radiating an energy. My images on the screen are amazing. I'm monochromatic, so it isn't a plethora of colours that attracts me, it's the power of black. The intensity of it which just blows me away.

Donna also finds that computer-based processes have enabled her to re-view her work in new ways. The translation from analog imagery to digital pixilations displaces some visual elements while highlighting others opening up further possibilities for viewing and interpreting the images.

> I will use adobe Photoshop as a means of quickly mocking up an idea because you can draw some lines, change the colours and have 10 versions very quickly to use as a jumping off point. To me that is a different use of the computer . . . you are drawing with a different pencil. That's really what it is and I'm not sure I would get there from sketching ideas. This idea of manipulating previous paintings and photos I've got and putting these filters over them that is interesting to me because it modifies an image you've already created or one you've done as a photo. It gives it a different meaning, a meaning you may not have considered . . . and it allows you to manipulate the image perhaps in ways that you wouldn't normally do.

Donna asserts throughout her descriptions of making art that she is tied very closely to the physicality of the hand rendered process. She maintains it is through the act of making that she is able to take risks and explore her dreams and thoughts. However, she rethinks this position, appearing somewhat contradictory when she says,

> I might take a bit more risk with computer drawings than I would with my own. I might go for the more dramatic . . . any time you're creating something there's the moment of getting it right. And there's the moment when you just let go of the image. Occasionally I can do that on the computer and say "what if I do this" and with the click of the button you can change the whole thing, and if you hate it you can change it back. It's a little harder to do with a sketch, you've got to peel it off and start the whole thing over again. So I can remember being free a couple of times more often using the computer. It depends if I can get myself into the "let go" mode . . . I can do it with the computer, I can do it with a pencil and I can do it with paint. I think it's a psychological breaking down of barriers.

Perhaps it is not so much a breaking down of barriers, but rather Donna's way of understanding the fluctuations between creating as poiēsis, and art making as production. *Poiēsis* is a form of becoming through the act of intuitive creating/making, while *production* is contextualized and molded by the intent of the artist and affected by the social processes inherent in the "surrounding order" (Griffins 1997). Both poiēsis and production are forms of technology.

The risks that Donna explores through computer manipulation are somewhat controlled by her own choices as well as the limitations of the computer program. While she claims she takes more risks using the computer for drawing, because of her ability to erase or delete those marks or applications she does not like, she does not have to make the same commitment to those marks as she does when working on paper or canvas. Donna knows that she can erase those unsatisfactory bits without leaving the traces behind. This ability to erase contests notions of the trace as evidence left behind by the maker (Krauss 1993). Donna has already stated that the marks she makes and the traces left in her drawings even after some marks have been erased, is evidence of her having made these marks. The marks are a form of commitment to the work. In Derridian fashion, they are the residue of her presence left in her absence (*cf.* Collins & Mayblin 2000:70).

Like Donna, Robyn also describes a difference she perceives in her ability to control imagery developed by computer processes because of the opportunity to erase those marks she does not want. She calls her form of commitment "seriousness."

> If I'm drawing or if I'm writing something down I take that a lot more seriously . . . maybe that's because of the speed and the ability to erase [when using a computer or surfing the Web] what came before. So if you're sitting and drawing or you're writing something out, the evidence is always there even if you try to erase it you still might be able to see it. Online [and in some computer programs] you go back and forth and you skip to the next thing. You can go back but you don't have to, you never have to face what came before. Physically, drawing is a lot less forgiving than being on the computer. You can erase things so quickly. Drawing on the computer is totally different for me than drawing with pen or pencil or painting. If I'm painting and I don't like what I'm painting, I have to put it aside and come back to it maybe two days to three days later depending on what medium I'm using. But with the computer, you can sit there for ten hours, and work faster because you can erase things immediately and go over top of things and layer and take it away if you don't like it. I just think it has to do with evidence.

Jack uses his computer to gain control over his processes for economic reasons. Mocking up possible colour combinations on the computer saves him money that might be spent on unwanted results using paint and canvas. While his art making is dependent on the spontaneity of his painting technique, his use of computerized colour sketches enables him to test-run his ideas, albeit on a small scale, reducing the risk of undesirable results that often happen from pouring paint on large canvasses.

> It gives me a general idea of what I'm up against. It might sound like I'm contradicting myself from one to the other, but I'm very spontaneous when I paint and if I want to do a large piece, say six foot square, it can also be very intimidating because it's a big space and there's a lot of materials that are going to be involved. There's definitely a cost to that, and sometimes that can be detrimental; it could stand in the way of your creative process because you don't want to make a mistake, you don't

> want to throw half a gallon of paint down and realize No!...And you end up painting over it with another half gallon or whatever the case may be. By the end of it you have a 200 lb. painting and it cost you $1000 to make. With a computer you can still be spontaneous and throw down colours and shapes and composition and then maybe look at it and think okay, that yellow bar, well maybe I'll move it down a bit so when you actually go to the bigger picture, you can work from it. Maybe not try to recreate it exactly, because that would defeat my purpose . . . it helps, but it's all new to me and I've just started to play with this idea.

Jack's desire to not make costly mistakes sets up a degree of resistance to his engaging the accidental in his traditional creative processes. He uses the computer to temper this resistance somewhat, enabling him to stretch his often limited material resources, as well as gain a safe degree of spontaneity in his painting procedures.

**Making in the space of an electronic *Other***

Throughout the conversations with all the artists, issues of control underlined their accounts of developing and making work using computer processes. While not as challenging to their making processes as the perceived loss of sensation and physicality, issues of being in control, losing control, or being under the control of the authority of an electronic or digital Other surfaced as a primary concern. Claire states,

> I don't give myself over soulfully. And maybe that's what it is. Maybe because it's all consuming . . . one thing I do have is I do have a tremendous power of concentration when I get up and running and I can become totally and absolutely absorbed in something to the point that I'm startled that the world is still here. When I'm in the computer maybe that's the thing that's going on, maybe there's that constant kind of push and pull about being taken over in a soulful kind of way in your pursuit and being guarded at the same time . . . there's that concern about loss of control on the part of the individual who happens to be me, of that complete giving over like you do when you have flow or whether that's impossible because it's about pieces of information as opposed to communication and ideas.

Through these descriptions Claire reveals two forms of different subjectivity. One is her guarded self which moves through new territories and technologies with caution and the second is her soul which the guarded self protects. Claire implies that it is through her soul that she can completely immerse herself in her art making practice.

Jin's issues of technological control are related to email communication. This control is rather ambiguous however. Jin's concern is that email senders have the control to constantly access him online, yet he has the control to choose whether he will accept and read the email.

> There's negativity on the side of technology - like email-wise, so many people are sending emails one to another and when you receive that many emails you just get bored of it. You don't even want to open them and you just want to delete them or avoid them.

Yet Jin also intimates that we have no choice in the fact that the world is changing and that we will be affected by those changes.

> We're having robots in the house now . . . it is kind of a confusing time to define because we don't know where this work [artists' work] is going to lead to yet. We don't know how things will change, it's really questionable.

The issue of a control mechanism or "Big brother" being present while the artist is creating might also be understood as a form of collective intelligence (Lévy 2000) or giant collaboration. The three older artists, Peter, Donna, and Claire all sensed another authority present when working on the computer. Donna describes it as,

> A sensation that you're not the only person in the room because there is the computer that exists or certainly the Web and all this digital imagery exists in a space out there somewhere in a world out there that you are

> connecting to through this little mouse that you click, but that's nowhere near the same feeling you get when the hand flows with the ideas of the brain. So to me, there's the layer in between you and what you're producing which are the computer guys who created the program you are using, the mouse controls, the language of Adobe Photoshop . . . I have the sensation of being distanced from the work, so what I'll do is I'll print the work off on the colour printer and bring it down here (to the studio) and cut it up, or draw on top of it, or do it in black and white and then I'll add my own paint.

Donna perceives that she takes her control back by marking over top of the work done in collaboration with the computer program, although she returns repeatedly to the computer program since it aids her in experimenting with her image making.

**The physical experience of art making and the digital lure**

In order to examine the physicality of making, I would like to consider that the act of making occurs within a particular space that is experienced and perceived by the maker through body and sense. Tuan maintains that as humans we experience space through the movements of our bodies and that sight and touch are "spatializing faculties" (2001:12). While I recognize that Tuan's perspective is based in humanist thinking that often borders on universals that can be problematic to postmodern projects, his theories regarding place, space and sensory perception are still useful for developing an epistemology that triangulates the body, space, and technology.

Two spaces in question here are the "real" space of the studio and the virtual spaces within the computer. How does the computer with its virtual space where sense and tactility are simulated affect the experience of making and creating? Although the studio-based creative experiences the artists described offer a virtuality in that the artists' engagement with their work is also outside their physical bodies and on a virtual plane, a condition mirrored in Foucault's sense of a virtual self (Batchen 1998), they are still connected with the "real" art materials and surface of the work in a tactile, physical way.

While engaging sensorially in their creative processes, many of the artists commented on experiencing a state of being that could be described as anaesthetic. This anaesthetic condition can be described as a "flooding [of] the senses" in a way that reduces an individual's awareness of what is going on around them (Buck-Morss 1995:22). It is so great that the artists experience a form of numbness that leaves them unaware of the physical surroundings outside of their relationship to the thing that is their work. At the same time, the tactile sense of this work is heightened, intensifying the physical relationship between the artist and their work. The traditional role of aesthetics as "being in touch with reality" reverses, and the effect of anaesthetics is such that the artists' senses are numbed, protecting them from the overstimulation of reality, a state that may inhibit their creative, productive processes (Buck-Morss 1992:18). The combination of heightened and reduced states of awareness and the dichotomizing effects of both aesthetic and anaesthetic conditions complicate the artists' art making experience. They go through an elevated sense of awareness to the interweavings of art making particulars such as texture, colour, and line while at the same time, they are "blocking out" distractions from the outside world. Together these processes facilitate the artists' immersing themselves in their work.

Buck-Morss cites suggestive information from neurologist Frederick Mettler. His claim is that there is "a contradiction between the reflective calm necessary to be creative (and to invent machines) and the destruction of this calm milieu by the very machines and increased productivity which the reflective mind creates" (1992:18). This contradictory condition is played out more so through the artists' descriptions of their experiences of researching on the Web than their accounts of their physical processes. However, engaging with new technologies has itself created distractions, some of which have drawn the artists away from their familiar ways of working manually. These distractions are not always negative as they challenge the artist to rethink their patterns and procedures leading them to reinvent new ways of working through media exchanges and integrations. I would however challenge Dr. Mettler's claims that the "reflective calm" necessary for creative work is destroyed by the distraction of machines. Instead, what is happening is more of a disruption of a calm condition, a disruption that provokes the artist to rethink their creative processes and open themselves up to adopting new procedures and technologies that are themselves embedded with different aesthetic forms.

Peter commented extensively on the importance of the physicality of art making and how that physical sensation is either lacking or altered in his digital experiences. Yet, at the same time, he is excited by the possibilities he gains through using his computer and is rethinking making processes in light of new technologies.

> There is a certain remoteness to it which fascinates me and frustrates me. I can work for hours on something [on the computer] and I lose a sense of time and scale. But for whatever reason, the work does not give me the physical satisfaction that I get coming into the studio and using a brush or a pencil. I'm tired at the end of the day [in the studio], physically tired as well as mentally tired. When working on the computer, I'm mentally tired, physically I'm not - I'm not stressed. Which also points to something that to me it's mesmerizing. I think what happens is that I'm in a trance in some respects. It isn't related to the creative space that I'm in when I'm working.

Peter indicates a form of aesthetic condition while working on his computer. This new kind of condition is different from his experiences of working manually because it lacks a focus on physical tactility and focuses more on the visual interactions that are appearing on the screen. In contrast, Peter describes the sensory blocks he has experienced while physically working with graphite and paper in comparison to using his computer.

When I create, I'm not conscious at all, I'm somewhere else and I know

> that all sorts of things - my metabolic rate goes up - I'm in a cold room I'll be warm. I'll come back from wherever that is and then I'm analytical. I'm starting to look at something and see it and analyze it. With the computer, there is that phase, but there's some lack of some sort of physical component- it's not physical. It is more like television, not that it's a passive thing, there's a definite interaction going on which I love.

Peter undergoes different forms of aesthetic conditions using both physical drawing materials and computer programs. Furthermore, he experiences the anaesthetic condition of blocking out distractions similarly for both types of creative practice. Like Peter, Jack also describes a form of losing himself while in the act of creating. He describes his loss of awareness of the world around him through a disregard for his own body temperature in relation to the room he is in. Jack explains his painting experience as a condition where he is,

> . . . pretty locked into things. I lose track of temperature, time, everything. I could sit in a pair of shorts in the middle of winter and not even be aware of being cold. It's a meditative state." He says however, that when he works at the computer "I'm definitely more aware of what's happening around me, I'm not as zoned out as when I'm painting . . . I'm not getting the same thing, it's almost like doing thumbnail sketches.

Working with a computer instead of paint has not developed as an aesthetic condition to the same degree it has for Peter. The intensity of Jack's focus in relation to creating is reduced when using a computer. For Jack, the tactility lost in the translation between physical and digital procedures affects his level of awareness to his work. Jack does not immerse himself in the digital processes in the same way he does when he is painting. It is not that he is totally distracted while working on his computer. Rather, he is less focussed.

Paradoxically, Peter claims that computer technology has "heightened my sensitivity to the physicality of art making. I don't think I really considered it before as much, now that I can take images and I can reproduce them." In this way, the aesthetic experience of one form of art practice has illuminated the more pleasurable experiences of the other. He continues this line of thinking by describing his relation to the screen.

> We haven't reached a level in the tactile aspect of computer technology. Things that I'm not happy with is the fact that the image is there "glowing" at me, but I can't get my hands on it, so perhaps we are in a transition stage . . . I can't touch the image, and on paper I can, I can smudge the graphite, I can play around with the paint. But it will be interesting, because maybe even with a tactile screen, it still won't solve the problem because it's not there - there is still an LCD or whatever it is between me and it. It's not your skin against the thing.

Manovich suggests all forms of screens, whether the screen created by a painting, television or computer screens, exist as "a flat, rectangular surface . . . intended for frontal viewing . . . in our normal space, the space of our body, and acts as a window into another space . . . the space of representation" (2001:95). He does distinguish however, that paintings can be viewed as classical forms of screens that present permanent static representations while computers are real-time screens which represent images that are continually updated (p.103). Yet, what Peter describes, as many of the others do also, is their "desire to touch" what is contained on the screen. It becomes a "gnawing void in [their] psyche. How can we verify anything without knowing that, if we really had to, we could put our hands to it?" (De Kerckhove 1997:132). Tuan maintains that "touching and manipulating things with the hand yields a world of objects" and that sight and touch, along with taste, smell, and hearing enable humans to apprehend "the world's spatial and geometrical character" (2001:12). It is through touch that these artists have learned to experience their making as familiar. Simulations of that tactility render an unfamiliar experience of space and the artists' location of their bodies in that space that is devoid of familiar objects. However, that may change for future generations of artists as new technologies change the ways in which they experience and interpret the world.

Jin likens his physical experience of making art to "creating and eating up a delicious meal . . . I like to do it spontaneously rather than preparing like many other artists . . . I approach making art like cooking." Jin's relationship to making is sensorily orientated and he regards the hands-on engagement as both sensory and spiritual.

> The hand is very spiritual - I don't think that's [art making] coming from your own hand, I think that it's coming from your soul, your intelligence, your passion, your expressions, your emotions. I treat my Mylar and my paper just like my skin. Skins are quite sensitive and irritable and delicate, yet they are a very important part of your body and once the paintings print on the surface, it is no longer my line because it is in combination with my soul. It's hard to explain if you're not an artist. If you're an artist, and you know what it's like, you get that sense when you're creating a body of work and you're so intense and when you couldn't even think about anything else because you are right in there - so it's like when you're watching a great movie and you feel like crying at that moment because you're right in the character. That's exactly how I'd like to describe what it's like when I'm creating a body of work. I like to be right inside, not to be thinking of it as an object.

Jin's description relates closely to the perceptible sensibility or aesthetic condition that Peter and Donna describe. Yet, through his experience of making, Jin also creates an abstract spatial experience that he embodies through "feelings, images and thoughts in tangible material" (Tuan 2001:17). The processes and ensuing created objects define Jin's art making in such a way that it takes on a physicality. Tuan suggests that objects or places, as in Jin's art making, "achieve concrete reality when our experience of [them] is total, that is, through all the senses" (p.18). In turn, this concrete reality invokes meaning. Although Tuan's treatment of spatial experiences as sensorial is framed in terms of universalities, it does nevertheless offer one way of thinking about Jin's making as a series of spatializing practices that are realized through his body which is totalized by the interrelationships between his hands, mind, and soul. These interrelationships are enacted by his senses.

Jin's engagement with computer technology intersects with his embodied sensorial space of making, prompting new spatial practices that in turn remap his sensory experience. He extends his capabilities through technology, while, at the same time, preferring his manually created markings.

> I thought about doing something in the future that my own ideas of drawings and paintings might become a little more figurative. So, I could digitize everything so I probably don't have to paint them myself and use all the colours and paints and save a lot of money and time . . . but I still want to have a touch of my own hand on top of the digital . . . at the end it all comes out of my own hand - it's just based on the computer for part of the pattern making, manipulating ideas and sketching ideas. It is totally my own, and because I like to do it the old-fashioned way.

Jin displays nostalgia for the fixed way of working, a nostalgia that Massey (1994:119) equates with the comfort of Being which is held by a sense of place grounded in past traditions, in this case the romantic notion of the artist in his studio. He does however speak of reorganizing the ways he might make art. This form of spatial reorganization can signal a shift in Jin's relationship to making as well as to the art objects he creates. Harvey contends that spatial reorganizations signal a shift in social relations, I am suggesting that these relations include the social connection of the artist to their work. Jin appreciates the facilities and opportunities provided by computer digitalization, yet the function his own hands play in the making of his work transcends for him any digital capabilities that are currently available to him. The reorganization of his practice has prompted Jin to examine his relationship to the making process and the role of the handmade art object within digital culture. What is important in this whole process is Jin understands that his thinking is grounded in digital culture and its increased opportunities of access; but what remains sacred to his making practices is his own hand.

In light of these questions, Jin contends that computer technologies will not alter the need for handmade art works. He claims that it is the emotion, the soul, and the evidence of something created by the artists' own hands that are the intrinsic values which make the work attractive and desirable.

Jin talks about "the soul" many times during his interview. For Jin, the soul is considered an aspect of the ways he attends to, or constitutes his self. It is his way of looking at his own self through the Platonic "other" eye, his soul. Jin employs this particular subjectivity of the self, this work of knowing about the self through self-formation, in a way that Foucault suggests illustrates his choice about his existence, a conception apparent in classical cultures (Rabinow 1984:361). This particular aspect of self, which is seen through the soul, is a virtual self in the sense that it is a self outside the self (*cf.* Rabinow 1984:367). In his critique of Foucault, Hall contends that this subjectivity seen as the "submission of the body through 'the soul' . . . constitutes a powerful way of rethinking the body's so-called 'materiality" (1996:13-14). In this way, Jin also makes his art within a virtual space that precedes computer culture, engaging a spiritual aspect of self, some of which is translated through the tactility of his hand-markings.

Donna reinforces Jin's and Peter's concerns about the need for touch and sensation while working. Tactility is important for placing her body in relation to the piece in progress and the performance that is inherent in her working processes. Donna experiences tactility in a much different way than Peter.

> I need the hand . . . body . . . brain connection. I need the sense of not thinking and letting it flow. I fully love Julia Cameron's way of looking at art as a
> spiritual act. Making art is a form of meditation in a certain way, you stop thinking, you can't do it all the time, you sit back and you critically analyze it and break it down or you go back, but there's a moment at which your hand and brush and the colours just dance and you're there, but you're not there. I cannot say that I've ever felt that I've danced with a computer mouse . . . it doesn't help you to produce images.

Julia Cameron's 1997 book *Artists' Way: A spiritual path to higher creativity* (Putnam Press) has influenced the working processes of many visual artists including Donna. While Donna's immersion in the physicality and spirituality of the act of making by hand is clearly articulated, her last comment however, "it doesn't help you to produce images" contradicts her earlier claims that the computer has enabled her to expand on her ideas, enabling her new ways to develop imagery. Donna's tension here is partly fueled by her expectation to feel euphoric in the act of creation which leads to the art product. Using a computer to produce imagery does not create this feeling for her, thereby leaving the creative process lacking or incomplete. Therefore, Donna appears to have difficulty seeing the printed versions of her computer generated works as finished pieces of art.

According to Heidegger, the "createdness" of a work is part of that work because it sets in place some sort of conflict that the artist brings forth through the production of the work (1971:62). Through the production process, for Heidegger, the conflict that is set in place draws the artist and the work into the origin of art and into Being. In Donna's case this is metaphorically re-enacted as a dance, where she is present in a place that is beyond language, opening her up to bringing forth "the unconcealedness of what is" (p. 69). Donna's dance is her way of becoming which transcends the equipmentality or usefulness inherent in the production of her work. Donna sees her digital procedures as efficient and productive in the arena of craftsmanship. Williams (1988) describes the historical definition of a craftsman or artisan as a "skilled manual worker without intellectual or imaginative or creative purposes" which is a contrast to the qualities possessed by artists (pp.41-42). He suggests that artists are engaged in creative and imaginative endeavours that became known in the 19$^{th}$ century as Fine arts. What distinguished artists from craftspersons in the past is the separation between "areas of imagination and utility." This however is contestable since craft work is indeed imaginative and creative. More recently, the boundaries between art and craft have become increasingly tenuous. The notes Donna gave me at the start of her interview emphasized that developing images using her computer was a great deal less personal for her than the hands-on making of painting and drawing. It distanced her from her work and she saw her ideas as processed, or translated through an input/output procedure that was "many levels removed from the hand-mind interaction." The communication between mind and body was indirect and the use of the mouse minimized the body movements involved in the image creation process which led to a much less emotional involvement in the overall process.

Jack's approach to painting is also grounded in his need for using his hands to work and to touch the thing.

> My passion lies in pushing paints around definitely. Hands-on working with materials could never be replaced by clicking a button or drawing on a plastic tablet . . . I've always worked with my hands you know whether it is a car engine or building things. I was a house painter for a long time. It's what I do here [at his job as a shipper]. I've always been more interested in building things, creating things, whether it's paintings or construction or moving things so I think the hands-on aspect of painting and mixing up your paint taking big trowels because I like to paint large trowels and stuff and spreading it around. I come from a pretty working class background my family, my grandfather was a bricklayer, all these construction sorts of things, so I think I have that mentality running through me.

Heidegger claims that "things move us bodily . . . Much closer to us than all sensations are the things themselves" (Heidegger 1971:25). Jack's relationship to things - the building and constructing of things are his way of becoming or autopoiēsis.

Donna's form of autopoiēsis is invoked by the haptic relationship she insists she must experience with the art piece, or, for her, it doesn't work as art. It doesn't in one sense produce meaning. Understanding the meaning of a work is so important to her own working processes. What she alludes to is related to Heidegger's concept of the "thingly" quality of a work. He maintains that "the thingly element is manifestly the matter of which it consists. Matter is the substrate and field for the artist's formative action" (1971:26). The physicality of the work, its thingly elements, opens up the work to stand in relation to the artist and "within the realm opened up by itself" (p.40). Donna suggests that work created by computer is lacking in physicality. She says,

> I see all these layers of electronics between me and my work and what's produced on the screen doesn't feel real to me, even when printed out it doesn't look the same because there's not the sense of me, my mark, my line. That's a whole different feeling.

The thingly element is confirmed by Donna's handmade marks. The act is essential in order for her to see the image as art. She described how often she develops an image on the computer situated in her bedroom, prints it off, then runs downstairs to her studio to add paint, crayon, graphite, ink or other mark making materials in order to really own the meaning of a work. In a fashion that Arendt called *Homo Faber* [man the maker] in her theories of the human condition, Donna's "technical applicability" of what she is doing is "a mere by-product of [her]endeavor" (1998:297). Her real quest in the making is to further her own knowledge of the world by developing new ways to construct meaning out of her interactions and interrelations with the things around her.

Robyn's relation to computer technology and making art is based in functionality and equipmentality. She attempts to separate the computer from other kinds of tools she uses for making art, but insists that there is sameness at some point. This sameness or lack of difference could be related to how Robyn uses the technology as a tool. It is a means to an end in the same way a pencil is. However, the end products are transformed as are the processes to reach those end products. Robyn's relationships to various kinds of tools differ because they are experienced differently through her own body movements and in the kind of space they inhabit within her working processes.

> It's definitely a tool in my art making, but while painting I'm obviously not using a computer. If I'm doing computer drawing which I do using a mouse, obviously it feels different from using a paintbrush. But, each thing feels different, a pencil feels different from a paintbrush or a ruler, they all feel different. I think that it is just another tool. I think that I feel that they're different, but I don't think that they really are different.

Robyn requires a physicality and material presence in her work beyond digitally conceived imagery. Like Donna, she is also attached to the *thingness* of the work, the properties that make it tangible and tactile. The thingness gives the work a form of reciprocity with its maker. The artists create and the thing they create emanates back a materiality to be experienced sensorially,

> I would never totally digitize my process of working. I wouldn't want my work to be entirely digital . . . I like physical objects. I like things you can pick up and feel and touch. I like the tactility, and I like the texture. I don't want things to just be what you see . . . my work will always have graphic elements in it or connected to something that happened on the computer, but I think that's unavoidable at this point.

Robyn is describing what Arendt suggests is the reification of a thought that occurs when making a work of art as opposed to fabricating things. She says that "works of art are thought things" and that the same hands that fabricate everyday utility objects, create art also (1998:169). The hands themselves give a living spirit to the work, a spirit that Robyn describes as manifested in the tactility. Again, like Donna, Robyn's "technical applicability" or procedures for constructing a piece of art are "a mere by-product of [her]endeavor" (p.297). Her endeavour is to construct meaning out of her interactions and interrelations with the world by making things that she can touch.

Robyn's computer use also includes designing Web sites starting with her own. This dimension of her creative production requires her to think about the formal properties (line, colour, texture, etc.) of art making in relation to the viewer's experience via the computer screen. She is asking questions that address the viewer's different kinds of experiences of space. While the screen is perceived as lacking tactility, it can be seen rather as reconfiguring the viewers' and the artists' tactile and spatial experience. Theories regarding haptical and optical properties of space are useful here in interpreting "knowledge of artistic space through the senses of touch and vision" (Lant 1995:50).

Lant uses Alois Reigl's nineteenth-century theories to illustrate the dichotomy between haptical and optical space. Lant distinguishes between "haptic objectivism" which is based on the artist working toward"objectivity in the tactile appearance" and "optical objectivism" where the artist strives for "objectivity of the visual appearance" (1995:63). The first is based on the sense of touch and a perceived nearness to the object/image. The second is related to visual qualities such as colour and light that are perceived from a distance. Distance is a relative term here as it could be applied to the space between the individual and a computer screen, a painted canvas, or a cinema screen. The physical art object facilitates a "nearness" because it can be touched. Digital images are perceived as more distant in that they are viewed without the opportunity for hand touch, in a way that Peter describes as, "your skin against the thing." Working across the gap that emerges from this dichotomy calls for a remapping of haptical and optical properties so that the perceived *far-ness* of digital images appears to come *closer* to the touch of physical art objects. Remapping sensory experiences can, as De Kerckhove suggests, provide the opportunity to rethink existing notions of spatial representations and "bring attention to new potentials and new areas of interest" (1997:134).

The ways in which one perceives the space of the computer screen are important to Robyn's work. She describes how she approaches web site designing and how she understands the principle of movement through virtual space,

> Right away I think of colour. I'm just trying to think about how this would be different if I was designing something online, and how I would use colour differently because I think it's one of the key things when you are looking at a web site. It's the same with physical art as well. There are obvious things that are different about how the viewer is interacting with what it is [Web site or painting]. When you're designing a web site you have to think about the person that is sitting there with the mouse in their hand and the keyboard in front of them and the screen, and how they're going to navigate through your site. Whereas art work, depending on what it is, whether it's painting, or it's sculpture or it's an installation, you're going to think about how your audience interacts with your work. With a painting, there's only so much you can do as an audience with a painting. If it's an installation and you've transformed an entire space, obviously how the person walks through your piece is going to be really important to you, the same way that interaction with a Web site is important in that way. So, maybe there is a lot of installation art that is connected to this whole notion of navigation using the computer because of space. Space has always been very important in art making for a very long time and I think the Web probably has affected that, has made it more important.

Robyn is experimenting with many different ways of being an artist within digital culture using computer technologies to her service and looking for ways she can connect with others. Her understanding about the rising importance of spatiality and technology has been theorised by intellectuals such as Casey (1996), Harvey (1990), and Massey (1994). Her own quest is not to replace or subvert material spatial experiences with computer simulations, but rather she is seeking ways to redefine the places for art making as spaces that as Massey suggests are "articulated moments in networks of social relations and understandings" (p.154). These moments are the dynamic meeting places of thought, idea, and of manifestations that produce representations through imagery. I will follow this line of thinking about space, place and making in relation to technological forms using Massey's conceptions of place and space more thoroughly in chapter five.

Claire perceives the physical relationship she develops through making as a coalescence of manual and digital ways of working. She attributes the intensity of experience to Csikszentmihalyi's (1997) concept of "Flow."

> The haptic space between me and the computer tends to disappear because I tend to be . . . in a different way. In both instances [working in the studio and at the computer] the haptic space disappears. In the computer, I feel like I'm, I don't know how to explain it, this is a tough one verbally. There's this physical and conscious state . . . What happens is that the computer kind of pulls me in almost a dark-sided kind of way. When I come back . . . it's a very absorbing kind of space. It is different and I'm having trouble trying to put it into words. When I work [in the studio] it's flow, and it's a beautiful place. When I come up from that place I'm almost startled that the house and the world are still here it's like a little flinch almost. And when I'm in the computer, it's like it has absorbed me in a way, maybe the flow thing is more of a marriage thing, more of a soul engaging thing, I don't know where you lose yourself, but in a different way . . . in the computer there's almost the feeling that you could get lost because this cyberspace thing is like a real entity in a way. An emotional entity, a psychological entity that's hard to explain. In flow there's a kind of a natural and rightness and every cell in your being, every atom, everything is right. It's not that with the computer that everything is wrong or anything is wrong, it's just maybe when you go into a virtual space you're not in flow. Flow is a more primordial part of our whole psychic, psychological, physical make-up. It's natural . . . It [the computer] almost pulls you into flow, but it's not flow it's something else and I don't know what to call it.

Claire describes an anaesthetic condition of "blocking out the rest of the world" that occurs while she is making by hand. This condition enables her to fully immerse herself in her work. She names that condition *Flow* because of reading about Csikszentmihalyi's theories. She also describes an altered state of aesthetics that she experiences while using her computer. However, Claire does not have a name for this condition. She experiences a new form of aesthetic condition prompted by immersing herself in work done on the computer and connecting to a less familiar space outside of herself and her studio. Working in this space does not prompt a numbing of the senses in an anaesthetic sense, but a heightened awareness of a different way of working that frequently involves an electronic Otherness. This particular condition for art making emerges from

Claire's way of working across the tension between aesthetics and anaestheics.

Claire is also experiencing the filtering of stimuli via a screen. The screen acts as a frame or window onto another space, separating "two absolutely different spaces that somehow coexist" (Manovich 2001:95). Manovich suggests that the screen that separates the viewer from the representation that they are viewing, acts aggressively, filtering out and "rendering nonexistent whatever is outside its frame" (p.96). Through the computer screen, Claire and the others experience a space that is cut out from the physical space of their studios, enabling them to focus on representations within this new space.

Additionally, Claire appears to be questioning the computer-mediated experience as leading to authentic experience that brings forth her being. For her, it is not a question of the thingness attached to art works, but rather the degree to which her being is brought forth and opened up during her complete involvement in making. Claire does not put up a resistance to the computer as a vehicle for creating, but rather, the computer is grounded in its functionality, its useful productiveness, which doesn't make it "wrong" it just doesn't facilitate openings onto the world in the same way that she connects to making through the tactile sensations of her hands touching the materials and the object. The computer creates a different set of dynamics that is based on simulations rather than physical "realness."

## Re-viewing and re-mapping

This chapter examined more closely three particular themes that emerged during the artists' interviews. These themes consist of the ways in which artists research ideas for making art, the ways in which artists' image producing capabilities were challenged and/or enhanced by digital manipulation, and the artists' attachment and commitment to the physicality of making art by hand and the tensions arising between the sensual tactility of physical art media and the seduction of digital manipulation programs. The artists all described how they 'gave themselves over' to the manual processes employed for making art, unconditionally and soulfully as they explored the sensorial physical experience of creating by hand. They spoke of a physical excitement as they immersed themselves in the hand-making of art objects. In contrast, they also claimed to be invigorated by the stimulating seduction of digital manipulation that offered them new possibilities for extending their imaginations. They described how they could be mesmerized by the possibilities offered by digital manipulation. However, they were also cautious not to give in to those new procedures completely through a full collaboration with what the three older artists alluded to was the digital Other.

It is clear from the conversations that the artists are looking for links between the older ways of working developed as hand makers of objects and the new found possibilities inherent in becoming digital. These links are not just technical, but also physical in form and feeling. What is at stake in becoming digital for many of the artists is compromising the tactile sensation they gain through making by hand. This contrast in their two experiential worlds presses the artists into rethinking and "remapping of [their] sensory life" to include both experiences that are private tactile sensations and the collective experiences mediated through computer or digital technology (De Kerckhove 1995:187). It is also these conundrums that foreground the body through a new heightened awareness of its presence in relation to technology and computer-based making. The stories are gateways to further discussions about space and place relationships that include the body within art making practices. They encourage us to consider a hybrid form of cyborgology in relation to artists working with diverse forms of technologies, especially crossovers between hand and computer.

# CHAPTER FIVE: EXCAVATING SPACES AND PLACES OF ART MAKING

## Problematizing the spaces for making art

In this chapter I expand on and clarify issues of space and place in relation to the *crossover phenomenon* illustrated by the artists' descriptions of making art in both physical and virtual environments. The artists appear to be working across differences in conditions for "making" and they are often caught in the act of translation that results in part, from their actions within three particular spatial realms. These three realms are: haptical space, narrative space, and paradoxical space. Two particular questions arise in relation to artists working across such spaces are: first, how are they affected by moving between radically different contexts; and second, how are their individual approaches to working across different spaces linked to measures taken by other artists in the study? The places and spaces for making art become problematized when artists work concurrently across both physical and virtual environments in developing and producing imagery.

Foucault suggests that *problemization* is set in motion when a multitude of factors are imposed on a "domain of action" provoking "a certain number of difficulties around it . . . To one single set of difficulties, several responses can be made" (Rabinow 1984:388-389). In this sense, contemporary art making has become problematized by new historical ways of thinking, acting and being that reconstitute their sense of "art", being an "artist" as well as their ways of producing art across different kinds of spaces and with very different technologies. Foucault argues that problematization "develops the conditions in which possible responses can be given" and also "defines the elements that will constitute what the different solutions attempt to respond to" (p.389). That is, the artists I studied perceptions of themselves as "romantically autonomous" hand-makers of aesthetic objects within a physical studio setting became problematized by their embracing virtual computer environments with template-based manipulation programs. This new context renders the artists more on the model of compositors and image replicators. A related question to those described is, to what extent and at what points do the artists acknowledge that these spaces for making art are distinct, and at what points do they attempt to blend these spaces together by working across the differences? To begin to answer these questions, the three spatial realms must be defined in relation to my analysis of the artists' interviews.

Haptical space is a "touch-space" that implies a nearness to the object or image an individual is viewing. It also implies a tactility that is experienced physically by the body. When artists make art by hand they are engaged in a haptic relationship with the thing they are making. This is recognized more easily when the artist is physically handling materials. Haptic space becomes problematized however when an artist uses a computer mouse, an experience wherein tactility apparently disappears behind the computer screen or is limited to minimal mouse gestures. As the shift to digital culture provokes a change in human sense perception, the physicality of touch- space is translated into a "shock- like" effect not unlike the effect of being bombarded by moving images that Benjamin attributes to cinematic hapticity. This occurs when the cinematic screen does not appear to have "actual tactile properties of its own . . . no modulated surface to feel" but the bombardment of images, or as Peter describes the "glow" of the image may be experienced in a physical way via the computer screen (Lant 1995:68; see also Benjamin 1968:223).

In contrast to haptic space, narrative space is defined in relation to stories and stories link places together. Narrative structures inherent in stories create "changes in space" by way of illustrating movements from one place to another (De Certeau 1984:115). The artists described in my study are like actors. Through their descriptions they act out the ways in which linkages are formed between different places and illustrate the "modalities' that specify the kind of passage leading from one to the other" (p.115). Their stories, whether relating to physical or virtual places, are all "spatial practices" or spatial stories (p.115). These narrative spaces illuminate opportunities for new spatial relationships that may stimulate artists to initiate hybrid forms of art making.

Paradoxical space on the other hand operates in ways "that would be mutually exclusive if charted on a two-dimensional map - centre and margin, inside and outside - are occupied simultaneously" (Rose 1993:140). De Lauretis concurs that these spaces are not "strung along a chain" but rather "they coexist concurrently and in contradiction" (cited in Rose 1993:140; also see De Lauretis 1987:26). The physical and virtual spaces the artists move across are paradoxical in the way they facilitate different kinds of procedures involving diverse technologies. The characteristics inherent in one form of technology influences the other forms in ways that appear to be contradictory at times. Yet, the artists adopt a multiple subjectivity that enables them "a productive mobility between differences" (Rose 1993:138). This enables them to continue working by hand and by computer in the development of the same image. They move back and forth within the paradoxical space translating anachronistic languages to digital interpretations and vice versa. While narrative spaces facilitate openings for the initiation of hybridities, those new hybrid forms, the cyborg for example, often propagate in paradoxical spaces.

The three spatial realms named above are experienced both individually and in combination as the artists work across different domains. These domains include the physical place called "studio" and the virtual realm of the computer both of which facilitate the development and production of images. The process of combining spaces and places that are both physical and virtual has emerged from a larger shift toward digitizing many cultural practices. This shift causes certain approaches to making art to be tied together as a way of developing possible solutions to the unsettled ways of thinking and acting caused by the shift. Not only does the process of problematization link diverse ideas and concepts together in ways that seek possible solutions to unsettling shifts, it also disturbs the artists' thinking about older forms of art making stimulating them to rethink what it means to be an artist in a digital culture. However, before examining each spatial form individually, I have redefined *the studio* as both place and space.

**Unfixing the artist's "studio" and reconstituting it as a fluid space**

Tuan asks whether *space* and *place* are "the environmental equivalents of the human need for adventure and safety, openness and definition?" (2001:202). This question has some relevance to the way Peter, Donna, Claire, Robyn, Jin, and Jack tell stories of finding familiar spaces for making in the art studio in contrast to the accounts of the venturesome collaborations they have with their computers. They tell stories about their experiences of exchanging and interchanging different procedures for making art in ways that Johnson describes as "the commingling of traditional culture and its digital descendants" (1997:8). When describing these procedures the artists often refer to a fixed location identified as their studios or working places. Given the context of digital culture they are now immersed in, the concept of "studio" becomes problematized as ways of thinking about the older model of the fine art studio and the hybrid version of a computer-based studio require an emergent place of working that ties both anachronistic and digital spaces together. The artists' reports are best seen as interpretations of their understanding of *the studio* as a historical construction that has become problematized by a cultural shift toward the digitization of practices such as art making. In some cases, these constructions involve a nostalgic perspective of what it means to be an artist within a fixed studio location conducting a practice invested with hand-making.

When using their computers to develop imagery, the artists are dislodged from familiar ground and transported to a space where the physical groundedness of manual working intersects with a new "virtual" mobility. It is within this in-between space that the tension between "fixity and mobility" occurs (Harvey 1993:7), sometimes rendering the artist vulnerable. The artists' own bodies become objects stretched across these different spaces, moving between the shelter of the familiar and a venture into the unfamiliar. They become very much like an exiled person trying to establish a new sense of home by developing new spatial patterns, ways of moving and working, seeking to establish a new comfort zone.

Becker contends that "the artist, writer and intellectual - like the exile - must learn to live with ontological insecurity" (1996:114). She says that the artist in this situation is always comparing what she experiences as existence in the present with what she remembers existing in the past by attempting to straddle multiple realities and dimensions simultaneously. The artist becomes caught between competing concepts of home or place as a fixed and rooted location on the one hand, and virtual places that are not tied to fixed notions of time and space on the other. These competing conceptions produce "differences between places [that] to some degree become antagonistic" (Harvey 1993:7). At this point, both the self and the landscape of place need to be remade. The artist becomes acutely aware of the competition between times when they perceive themselves to be fixed to one locale, and other occasions when they are mobile and unconstrained (p.7).

Massey, however, maintains that places are determined by the "interactions which they tie together" (1994:155) and involve our experiences of those interactions. In this way, places are really social processes. Considering this, the artists' studios are not really fixed but rather are themselves processes of interaction, thought and making. This definition offered by Massey provides an avenue for breaking away from inside/outside oppositions in relation to place which tend to convey "a common association between penetrability and vulnerability." Massey says such oppositions invite anxiety about the "invasion of newcomers" into a circumscribed place, and, in the case of the artists, the invasion of new technology into their established studio places (p.155).

The studio place can also be viewed as a process that ties together the many forms of interaction the artists employ for developing visual representations about the world. Thus, the studio place may be a room in a building, a dining room table, or a computer. For many artists, particularly women with family obligations (I include myself in this group), or artists with very limited resources, the studio place has rarely ever had a fixed notion of place because its changing location has been governed by constantly shifting social, economic or domestic factors. In many cases, then, the studio place, "is more an event than a thing to be assimilated to known categories" (Casey 1996:26). It is a space where "things happen." In this way, Casey suggests, places depend on the activities that constitute them. The studio *happens*. It is a place because of the process of making art. The making constitutes a cluster of relations, social and otherwise, which solidify the experiences of an artist at that moment.

## Reconstituting the haptic spaces of art making

The artists I interviewed appear to experience three particular spatial realms. The first of these spatial realms to be examined here is *haptic space*. The artists in my study privilege their physical bodies as sensory mediators within their art making processes. They describe the relationship they have to the materiality of the work they are making by hand as grounding them in the physical and tactile world. Through touching and manipulating an emerging art object, they are experiencing a haptic form of spatiality. The artists describe how *touch* is integral to the making of the object at particular times. For example, Donna, Claire, and Jin suggest that they do not always see their work as whole images, but rather as tactile surfaces. Moreover, Peter says that while he appreciates the "power of black" he sees in his digital drawings on the computer screen, he cannot touch the black and smudge it the way he can with his graphite on paper. When working on the computer, touch is largely exchanged for sight.

Haptic space exists between our hands and our bodies as we reach out and touch the objects we encounter every day. It is also considered by Paterson as *touch space*, a space "more proximal than visual space"(2000:2). Haptic space is a reciprocal space. He maintains that,

> the promise of tactility is there in showing how the world touches us as well as our ability to touch the work [of art] itself. Haptic experience is therefore bi-directional. Its reciprocality stemming from the possibility of our touching an object, a surface, while simultaneously producing affects, of the object touching us (p.3).

Paterson argues that sight alone does not provide sufficient information about texture, mass, volume or surface of things we encounter. It is through touch that the encounter and experience of object and body in space are realized. Haptic space designates spatial feeling through the body. Touch is important to sensing space and place and it is this haptic experience that researchers are studying so intensely in relation to *virtual reality*.

The artists exchange a privileging of their bodies through tactility for a prioritizing of visuality via the computer screen. There the eye and the mind take priority over the hand and touch. In a Baudrillarian sense, the act of making is interiorized within the screen, exchanging the exteriority of the physical studio space for a "media space" (Kellner 1989). Kellner claims this exchange renders the eye and the brain as a kind of information processing system which is intended to replace "human practice and techne and [poiēsis] alike" (p. 6). This approach to using computers in particular typifies the cautionary overtures of Peter, Donna, Claire, and to some extent Robyn, toward replacing hand fashioning with digital processing. However, synchronizing the movements of a computer mouse while developing an image on a screen requires more than simply information processing. Drawing and painting an image via the computer entails very specific, albeit limited, body movements, where the hand is coordinated with the eye in the service of the mind. For the artist, this requires a different kind of spatial poiēsis (I am retaining Heidegger's spelling) that is less like a performed dance, and more like synchronized swimming.

In this case, the changing sense ratios across different technological spaces affect the artists' whole perception of the world, and the way they are able to manifest representations of that world. The artists are beginning to recognize the ways in which they exchange sensory ratios as they shift their work between hand and computer. However, the question still arises as to how they compensate for a loss of touch when using computers. Perhaps Benjamin's theory about the shock of the image generating a physical experience is useful here. Peter implies that there is a physicality in the "glow" of the image and "the power of black" presented on the computer screen. This represents a new form of hapticity that is yet to be named. It requires a rethinking of how tactile and visual "shocks" are refracted and translated across material and virtual domains.

Manovich says that "reality is cut by the rectangle of the screen" (2001:104). He includes the rectangular screens of painting, film, television and computers. He suggests that this cutting out and framing situates the viewer in two spaces: "the familiar physical space of her real body and the virtual space of an image within the screen" (p. 104). Historically, the screen has demanded that its viewers be fixed in space in order to see the image before them. This is the case in film, TV, and the computer image. Even the viewer of paintings is fixed in space in order to experience the image (p. 105). Making and viewing however, can be two distinct practices when engaged with physical materials in hand making processes. Making images via a computer screen begins to merge these two practices which are dependent on the fixed position of the maker as also a viewer in front of the screen. When the artist is hand making a work, they are not necessarily fixed in position but have the opportunity to move around and across "the screen." They rely on touch, performance and body movement as they interact with various materials while developing the image.

The artists I interviewed work in both physical, haptic spaces of bodily movements and creative performances, as well as virtual spaces of representation within various kinds of screens (this includes painting). It is only when manual artists lay down their materials, step out of the performance of being an artist and into the role of a viewer, that they become fixed in front of the screen. There are exceptions to the mobility of the artist I am describing here. Manovich's (2001) historically based research of perspectival drawing machines of the Renaissance suggest that draughtsmen were required to stay still in a fixed position while drawing the image (p. 105). It appears here that it is machines that tend to fix the artists in position while creating. When the artist works digitally on a computer, they start from a fixed position, viewing their digital manipulations as they appear on a screen that depends on light transmission instead of tactile sensation. Performativity and touch are exchanged for control and calculation. In this process the computer screen filters out the sensation of touch transforming the spatial expression from haptical to optical (*cf.* Lant 1995:49 & 68).

While the physical and virtual worlds here appear to have no relation to each other, Manovich suggests that "the virtual world is synchronized precisely with the physical one" (p. 111). In this way, the artist creates an image in both spaces that may appear visually similar, but palpably different such as Peter's black and white drawings in graphite and in pixels. The image is created within the virtual screen of the computer. In the case of several of the artists studied, this image will later be manifested again through the material object of a painting, drawing, or printout on paper in the physical world. Increasingly, the artists I studied were interested in merging digital and manual procedures in the service of an end product that can be touched again.

Additionally, Manovich notes that we are progressively entrenched within a culture of screens: ATM machines, airport information terminals, and food store cash registers to name a few. While this may be the case, many individuals, especially artists, are working to re-emphasize the physicality of our environments by calling attention to the sensory experiences of touch. If our western culture is to inhabit both real and virtual spaces comfortably at the same time, we must look to new ways of inscribing our bodies as mediators of spatial experiences that are both physical and virtual within the multiple spaces of representation.

**Spatial stories**

The second spatial realm I am exploring in relation to the artists' interviews is narrative space. The artists tell stories that involve spatializing practices which invest their bodies into the discourses of space and place (De Certeau 1984:116). While the studio *place* may imply a certain degree of stability, the space of making is fluid. This space is a process that is driven by a multiplicity of transformational moments, which emerge out of an intermingling of the artists' experiences within social, cultural, technological, historical, and autobiographical contexts. These transformational moments impose on the artists' ways of looking, making, and performing creative acts.

Stories, De Certeau suggests, "carry out a labour that constantly transforms places into spaces or spaces into places." He says that stories "organize the play of changing relationships between places and spaces" (p. 118). The artists' conversations I studied here are plays of changing relationships between the places and spaces of their making. The idea of a play suggests that they are actors performing acts of making as in Donna's dance with her paintbrush or Jack's pouring paint onto large canvasses on the ground, and then actors telling a story. In the case of the artists interviewed, the stories illustrate the comminglings of traditional and digital culture.

The artists tell stories about what they do in different kinds of places. They describe what it feels like when they are manipulating different materials while creating an image in their physical studios or the anxiety of navigating through unknown areas of the Web. They also tell stories of working across different spaces at the same time. Donna relates the story of how she changed the colour tones in an acrylic painting after seeing how "bright" they appeared in digital form on her computer. Working across the physical and virtual spaces created by the image, Donna found a new space of making. Donna's story describes the space of difference that emerged for her between the physical work and its digital representation. This represents the transformational moment of viewing her image in two different states and then her actions that followed.

Art making is a spatializing practice of representation (De Certeau 1984; Harvey 1990). Every story is a "spatial practice" (De Certeau 1984:15). This applies to every representation whether produced in physical or virtual form. Like map making, creating images and visual representations "collate on the same plane heterogeneous places, some *received* from a tradition and others *produced* by observation" (De Certeau 1984, p. 121). Meta-narratives of modern Western art history offers the artists a foundational story of conventions and suppositions from which they may choose to operate when making art. This particular foundation affects the spatial practices constructed by artists in ways that authorize a distinct set of relations in each instance of art making (De Certeau 1984:125). However, this modernist authorization is challenged as a fixed foundation when confronted and fragmented by the multiplication and diversification of changing technological contexts (De Certeau 1984), such as when forms of virtual mobility impinge on older, established spatial practices.

De Certeau suggests that inscribing the body onto space through movement and action (making) always "organizes a *here* in relation to an *abroad*, a 'familiarity' in relation to a 'foreignness" (p. 130). What is closer often emerges as more familiar. Donna says that she feels "distanced" from the works she creates on the computer. They are not familiar to her touch. Spatial stories emerge through the experiences of particular spatial relations. As a result, artists begin to develop conceptions of space that develop out of *familiarity* such as working in the physical studio place, out of *foreignness* evident in the Web navigation stories of Claire or the "Otherness" of computer programs described by Donna and Peter, and the differences in between. Differences are found in stories of concurrently working by hand and computer to produce an image. These stories open up new forms of space that affect the processes employed within the making place, prompting new spatial stories to emerge. Out of these stories hybrid forms of making may be initiated.

**Working through the paradox: Making art in both manual and digital spaces**

The fusion of technology and culture has "been a part of human experience since the first cave painter, but we've had a hard time seeing it until now" (Johnson 1997:2). The changing technological environment has caused interruptions to individuals' routines, yet there "is a kind of knowledge to be found in those interruptions" (p.3) that should make all of us think twice about everyday practices that appear to be second nature. Johnson says that it has only been recently that our Western culture has begun to recognize the "patterns" and "contours" of the changes and interchanges between art, technology and information (p.4). Moreover, as the computer is accepted as a medium for making art and producing images, it increases its ability to change the thought patterns of the users, and, as a result, change their perspectives on the world (p.50).

Similar to the ways in which the perspectival technologies of artists like Alberti and Leonardo changed "the spatial language of European painting," as well as "the role of the artist itself" (Johnson 1997:214), computer imaging programs such as Photoshop have transformed what it means to create, reproduce, and disseminate imagery in a digital culture. The act of artistic *making* using a computer, again changes the languages required for developing images and the spatial relationships between the artists and their work. Furthermore, anachronistic methods of creating visual representations, the traditional role of artists, and the terms on which they *make* art are called into question.

The technologies of perspective effectively grounded painting in "the physical, lived reality of the human body" as it provided a singular point of view from a fixed human standpoint (Johnson 1997:214). The technology of perspective not only changed the visual space of the artist's picture plane, but socially reconstructed the individual's view of the world through visual representations. However, this grounding in singular perspectives, as illustrated in the interviews with Peter, Donna, Claire and Jin, has been disrupted and reconfigured in relation to the multiple perspectives enabled by the computer. The physicality and depth of images afforded by optical perspective are experienced quite differently when the image is translated to digital form. Not only does the tactility that is more recognizable in handmade objects disappear, but the digital image is potentially malleable into a multitude of perspectives simultaneously.

The spatiality of making the work has changed, as has the artists' thought patterns and approaches of how they develop and produce images. In some cases their own assumptions about what kind of images constitute the label of "art" and hold monetary and/or aesthetic value within the Fine Art discipline, are contested. Johnson offers that just as perspective painting helped initiate the Renaissance, "information space is the great symbolic accomplishment" of this era (p.215). Now individuals, such as those I interviewed, have to come to terms with these new spatial arrangements in such a way that the influences and range of dominant and comfortably established media forms become perceptible within their practices. This change in perception potentially disrupts their old assumptions and conventions. The artists adopt new ways of making art in a paradoxical space that provokes them to work across the differences they perceive between handmade and digital processes of image production. Donna does this when she "works into" or on top of her digital images with more traditional artists' materials such as crayon and paint.

Collins maintains that technological instruments such as TVs, VCRs, and computers transform the postmodern spaces of offices, living rooms, and in the case of my research, artists' studios, into "instant ad hoc archives" where "juxtapositions are a matter of perpetually reconfigurable random access" (1995: 3). The juxtapositions that Collins refers to are provoked by the intersections of history, culture, technology, and popular taste within information-spaces. As well, the intersections between anachronistic and innovative practices are being reconceptualized as cultural producers increasingly find new ways to develop exchanges and interrelationships between old and new media forms within reconfigured spaces. In light of this, Collins asks how individuals are developing "a satisfactory sense of identity by locating themselves, spatially and historically, in reference to the array of information and information technologies?" He also wonders what is happening to "the relationship between tradition and innovation" as a result of these new information spaces? (p.29)

Robyn and Jin have a strong sense of identity as artists who continually inform themselves about the world through the Internet and the Web. They are able to comfortably commingle their roles as artist/electronic information gatherers with the role of artist/makers. They display a kind of information savvy, a "streetlevel" confidence (Collins 1995:10) that enables them to embody a cultural currency within their work, handmade or otherwise. In fact, Robyn's work is about information and the way it proliferates through various visual forms. Information is her subject matter. As young artists, they see these information spaces as a form of community, a localization of the global. They both participate in numerous communities that include artistic, musical, and informational venues across a variety of social relations and spaces.

While the perception of time-space compression has caused anxiety for many (Harvey 1990; Jameson 2003; Tomlinson 1999), Robyn and Jin embrace the opportunities afforded them by a new access and mobility. They are able to move quickly across the speedy information spaces of the Internet, yet at the same time, work through much slower anachronistic processes of hand making in order to produce imagery. They can work in both spaces simultaneously by keeping in touch with the world through the immediacy of the Internet, while using time-consuming procedures for making art.

Collins' questions, however, are not easily answerable for many older artists. Peter says that as an artist he feels he lives a "schizophrenic existence." This is because he is still in a transitionary stage of coming to terms with the changes that are occurring in his approaches to making as well as his relationship with the computer as a medium for acquiring and reconceptualizing information. He says he is "not completely on one side or the other" implying an in-between ness to his situation.

The role of the artist as maker has been reconfigured as a result of the development and engagement of new information spaces. A large part of this reconfiguration is due to the ways in which, as Lash suggests, the artist's studio has become more like a laboratory. In the past, the studio was considered a space that was "lifted out from routine forms of life" as an "autonomous" artist created "pure art." Similar to the change in scientific laboratories, the pure art form "descends so to speak, from its pure autonomy" to become a form of techno-art, just as everyday social relations rise to become forms of laboratory life where science, art and society "become technological" (2001:114).

The "work," or as Lash maintains, "prototype" produced within the newly reconfigured studio "seriously flies in the face of the idea of genius of the autonomous artist and scientist. This is because it is collectively produced" (p. 114). Prototypes however imply singularity, a model that may be reproduced. Images created in a "digital studio" may be manipulated and reproduced so the model becomes multiplicitous. The work in the digital studio is a pluralized prototype within a network of images. It becomes a *Text*. The "Text poses problems of classification." It is the "movement of a discourse" and acts as an "activity *of* production" (Barthes 1977:157). Barthes contends that "the Text is always *paradoxical*" (p.158). Peter has recognized this way of making art as a form of text production, a way of "playing" with images in collaboration with computer programs (p.158). He begins to exchange older patterns of sketching and gesturing for new ways of producing knowledge through the creation of a multitude of digital prototypes that are not easily classified as singular pieces, a series of interchangeable parts of a larger project.

*Homo Faber* divided things made by hand into items created for utilitarian purposes, and things, or rather art works, that were to be appreciated for their manifestation of thought. Through the mediation of a computer, a utilitarian appliance of the information age, the *thought things* are reprocessed through a digital interchange and manifested as test-runs of what will eventually be the physical representations of the artists' everyday interactions in the world. Currently, Donna and Jack both use the computer to test out ideas before working with physical materials on a larger scale. They use their computer prototypes as trial experiments for the "real" art pieces they will come to make. For both, the computer provides a test laboratory for playing with images that later are incorporated into representations to be produced in their traditional studio places.

Both Donna and Jack have delegated their art making activity to two types of spaces. One initiates a utilitarian kind of image development using the computer and the other inspires the actual production process of making art by hand. These activities occur in two different places which appear to support different kinds of making spaces, yet they coexist together in the paradoxical spaces of the artists' practices for the purpose of developing and producing art works. The two places may appear to be distinct in the way Donna and Jack approach image making, but they are tied together in ways that move the artists toward their desired results.

Both Donna and Jack commented that the "samples" they produce using the computer would otherwise not be possible through hand renderings or preliminary sketches. This perception may have transpired because the computer enables an ad hoc archive of information in a myriad of forms that the artist can access randomly as they create using digital procedures (Collins 1995). This accessibility is not present when drawing by hand alone and brings in to focus one of the challenges that anachronistic technologies and procedures face in the new age of access and information.

Those of us engaging in digital technologies will increasingly witness older media forms and practices "seeking to reaffirm their status within our culture as digital media challenge that status" (Bolter & Grusin 2000: 5). This at first may appear as a territorial struggle. However, it is more the practice of remediation where one medium is represented within another. When traditional perceptions of image making procedures are problematized by the possibility of multiple representations via digitization, or artists question how using one medium might be more appropriate or efficient over another, then they are engaging in what Bolter & Grusin name "acts of remediation" (2000:44). In some ways new electronic versions of an image are an improvement over handmade renderings. However, in their discourse "the new is still justified in terms of the old and seeks to remain faithful to the older medium's character" (p. 46).

Examples of these forms of remediation are the manners in which digital imaging programs such as *Paintbox* and *Photoshop* borrow from traditional media practices of painting and photography, or the Web assumes "pages" as a way of organizing units of information. In both cases, the computer versions retain a connection to the traditional forms, while at the same time improve on them, making them more efficient. Yet, there is a translation process going on here that some artists are engaging in more actively than others. For example, Donna fills in the gaps left by the translation of digital images to hand-drawing by adding her paint and crayon marks on top of the digital. Jack tries to re-imagine digital images in terms of physically painted canvasses.

Remediation requires that artists reconsider the particular qualities of different media and how they become evident within the process and product of making art. The artists engage in the remediation process when they accommodate both familiar, traditional techniques and digital technologies as interrelated parts of their practices. Moreover, they begin to acknowledge the paradoxical spaces of image production and open up the possibility of propagating hybrid forms of art making.

## New inscriptions

Rogers (1995) and Roland (1990) caution artists and art educators that they cannot simply superimpose the language and actions of analog/hand rendered methods of image production onto new digital forms. Both practice and production require a new language for remapping spatiality as manual and digital procedures cohabit the making spaces and places of artists. As a result of these new spatial arrangements, *works* become *Texts* as artists play with multiplying images and pluralizing meaning. Their perspectives on their work changes, refracting across physical and virtual domains, often losing or gaining something in the translations. The artists' stories evolve as they embrace new ways of making in exchange for the resistance they once may have had as they acknowledge new forms of hapticity that are still unnamed, yet physically experienced on different levels.

In an era that privileges multiplicity over singularity, artists are poised to take on different roles simultaneously as conceptions of making and creating are challenged on many fronts. The fact is that the hand maker of traditional fine art is now transforming into a new hybrid figure within digital culture. The six artists I interviewed have entered emergent spatial realms where their making procedures demonstrate new kinships between themselves and their computers.

Chapter six examines this new hybridity beginning from Heidegger's theories of *Handwerk* as ways of becoming through hand making. It then explores the possibilities of cyborg identity as a reconceptualization of becoming via Donna Haraway's (1991) cyborg manifesto. I take the idea of *cyborg* as a way for the artists, as Haraway suggests, to form a kinship with machines. While there are many questions that arise from this new kinship, her manifesto provides openings into new possibilities for making art that embraces the pleasures of the digital.

# CHAPTER SIX: THE EMERGING HYBRID CYBORG ARTIST

## Things Men Have Made

*Things men have made with wakened hands, and put soft life into are awake through years with transferred touch . . . for this reason, some old things are lovely . . . with the life of forgotten men who made them.*

## Things Made by Iron

*Things made by iron and handled by steel*
*Are born dead, they are shrouds . . . Till after a long time, when they are old and have steeped in our life . . . They begin to be soothed and soothing; then we throw them away.*

D. H. Lawrence (De Sola & Roberts 1993)

These short excerpts from two poems by D.H. Lawrence illustrate an antiquated romantic perspective regarding the relationship between humans and machines, particularly in regards to the act of making things. They speak to opposing views, where working by hand enables the maker to give life to materials through touch, whereas things that are manufactured by machines suffer a cold and disposable existence. Humans and machines are seen as very much at odds with each other, a perspective that has continued in some respects, into postmodernity. That said however, artists who are using their home computers to reconceptualize and re-imagine their hand working abilities in different ways are becoming a new community of hybrid art practitioners. These artists are beginning to work in collaboration with, or as Haraway (1994) suggests, joint kinship with machines in order to realize new ways of working and being. This chapter will examine the importance of touch in relation to traditional perceptions about artists working by hand, and then disassemble these assumptions and relationships through a cyborgian perspective that foreground computers within traditional image production and art making.

## The essence of *Handwerk*-ing

*Making*, as an integral part of art practice, involves the body and the hand within a haptic space that surrounds the work that is being made. The hand acts through a form of thinking that manifests representations, and actualizes the space of those representations. Paterson (2000) maintains that "hands as mediators, as mediating between the body and its surrounding space, are what form and maintain the idea of touch-space, the proximal types of near body space that stands in relation to visual space" (2000:5). For artists, this near body space is enthralling, captivating, and an integral part of the work during its development into thoughtful things of both bodies and minds.

When making by hand, the artist reconsiders their materials and surfaces in relation to their bodies every time they begin. Each approach to new work requires the artist to revisit, and learn again, the body-to-easel, or body-to-canvas, or body-to-paper relationship, and reconceptualize the space that is created within that particular moment of working. To learn, Heidegger maintains, "means to make everything we do answer to whatever essentials address themselves to us at a given time" (1968:14). When the artist endeavours to learn anew through their making, they must know about the making beyond applications and techniques. They must learn to answer to the essentials of what it means to make things by hand, by the way the hand touches and gives form through that touch, by the way it thinks before the mind, and its responsibility in manifesting particular representations of the world regardless of the material medium used, or kinds of renderings displayed. Above all, the artists must see their learning and making as an immediate relatedness to the world that extends beyond practice and skill.

In accordance with Heidegger's thinking, concepts of learning, particularly within the sphere of learning to make by hand, instill the artists' need to consider making as an act of relating to the world, not simply a series of procedures used to manufacture a product. The artists must answer to all the ways in which paint, graphite or ink can manifest visual representations about the world and effect meaning, and the ways in which a myriad of gestures and marks are the conduits for these manifestations. Heidegger calls the hand "a peculiar thing" (p.16). He contends that its essence lies far beyond its place as part of a bodily extremity that allows us humans to grasp other things. The hand and its essence (among other things) are what distinguish humans from other animals. Moreover, Heidegger insists, "only a being who can speak, that is think, can have hands and can be handy in achieving works of handicraft" (p. 16). For example, the hand extends itself, gestures, signs, speaks and manifests thought through things deemed handiwork. The essence, and "all the work of the hand is rooted in thinking" and its relatedness to making and dwelling in the world (p.16).

The hand is the mediator of thought within the act of making work and actualizing the space of representations. It is also the conduit for human touch-space relations to things and the material world. Derrida claims that Heidegger "in effect binds thinking, and not only philosophy, to a thought or to a situation of the body" (1987:171).

Derrida responds to Heidegger's notions of *handwerk* and *the thinking hand* in his essay "Geschlecht II." Derrida says that the hand has a double vocation. He argues that the hand holds on to speaking in ways that "show [montrer] or point out (zeigen, zeichen) and to give or give itself" (p.174). He claims that the essence of this argument is in the "opposition of *giving* and *taking*: man's hand *gives and gives itself, gives* and *is given*, like thought or like what gives itself to be thought and what we do not yet think" whereas an animal can only grasp or take (p. 175). In this way also he says, the hand as a mere appendage can only grasp, yet as a thinking hand involved in *handwerk*, the hand has access to an "essence" of being (p.175). The "giving hand" appears throughout the artists' texts as the essence of their making that is beyond functional production and the maneuvering of tools. The hand is *given* by the artists through their hand-makings. Derrida's diametric condition of giving and taking as outlined above is useful for distinguishing between acts of utilitarian production and acts of *handwerk* or extending "the gift" as the hands show themselves (p.173 & 176).

For visual artists, the hand is the point from which they make. It embodies the space of representations through touch. The hand is the mediator between artists' bodies, "things, space, and [their] world" in such a way as to "engender a difference" between visual encounter and physical engagement (Paterson 2000:7). That being said, if the hands are the mediating organisms between artists, their representations, and the rest of the world; how then, does the use of a computer alter this kind of mediation? How are the artists *refashioning*, as Bolter and Grusin (2000) suggest, their creative practices in ways that see hand making reconceptualized as computer manipulation?

Bolter and Grusin maintain that remediation is a way an individual reforms an older media into a newer type as a way of improving on the former. The process is one of re-purposing where the gaps or deficiencies of the older form are improved upon by the new media (2000:59). They claim this process also "offers a means of interpreting the work of earlier media" since we know media through a "genealogy of affiliations not a linear history" (p.55). That being said, if the cyborg is considered to be an incorporation of machine and human, can the hand be reconceptualized digitally and electronically as a conduit for computer aided thinking? Does this form of remediation lead to discovering new ways of art making and being an artist? What I am proposing here, is that by remediating the notion of handwork, and reconceptualizing the spatial references of the hand, artists can enter into, and make art within the realm of the cyborg.

**Introducing artists to the cyborg realm**

In her legendary work "The Cyborg Manifesto," Donna Haraway (1991) proclaims that "we are all chimeras, theorized and fabricated hybrids of machine and organism; in short, we are cyborgs. The cyborg is our ontology" (1991:150). It is not entirely clear in her account as to whether the cyborg is a metaphor, a fiction, an entity, or an identity. However, Haraway presents the cyborg as ironic, having a double-ness that opens up opportunities albeit in a paradoxical space while provoking a disrupted form of action and resistance through its darker, "blasphemous" side. Yet, Haraway's form of cyborgology still "opens the way for an imaginative leap to speculate about the political and epistemological possibilities for using technologies to develop alternative connections with each other and the life world" (Sofoulis 2001: 4). She presents "an imaginative resource suggesting some very fruitful couplings" (Haraway 1991:150). The cyborg provides a vocabulary for a particular way of being in the world and a new form of autopoiēsis. It also lends an immediate existence to the new hybrid form of a hand/machine maker required by digital culture. The cyborg entertains a fearless "joint kinship" (p.154) between human and machines in a way that the machine can enter into a handmade world. A joint kinship with the computer enables the artist in a cyborg realm to see from the perspectives of both humans and non-humans, in a kind of double vision of physical and digital worlds entwined.

The cyborg is a fractured subject, unafraid of "permanently partial identities and contradictory standpoints" (p. 154). The cyborg lives with both dominations and with possibilities, opening up new channels for specific hybrid identifications. The "fictional mapping" (p. 150) of the cyborg onto the artists' ways of becoming, affects their engagements with computer technology by offering them an opportunity to break down dualistic borders between the hand workings and the computer workings of their practices. The artists' new found double vision invoked by working within the realm of the cyborg also offers them the possibility of seeing a perspective other than the "deepened dualisms of mind and body, animal and machine, idealism and materialism in the social practices, symbolic formulations and physical artifacts associated with 'high technology' and scientific culture" (p. 154). With the termination of these dualisms, the domain of the cyborg empowers the artist to commingle and couple with the computer in an intimate relation of "mind, body, and tool," arousing a pleasure in the hybridity of the plurality formed with a nonhuman (p.165). The artist and nonhuman computer exist in kinship for the pleasure of making.

Haraway suggests that communications tools such as computers are "recrafting our bodies" and blurring the boundaries between machines and organisms (p. 164). The handwork of the artist no longer relies on the touch-space enabled by a sensing skin, but rather by an intimate relation to visual representations imagined through a pulsing of the quasi-prosthesis of the computer mouse. This is not a rebirth of the hand maker, but a regeneration of the maker as a hybrid who has not emerged from any distinct origin, but rather develops from the double vision inherent in the entwining of humans and machines. As Haraway notes, it is a condition that has heightened "our sense of connection to our tools" (p. 178). Peter implies this new relationship when he suggests that the computer enables him to work differently, sometimes more efficiently or "controlled" than by hand alone. He also says that working by computer has "heightened" his sense of physicality when he works by hand.

In terms of handwork, the relatedness of the artist to the machine is beyond notions of "utility" and "application" in ways that answer to a new sense of connectivity to the essence of the tools, as well as ways of exploring a reconceptualized form of making. By working within the realm of the cyborg, artists' encounters with their computers cease to be in opposition to their hand working engagements. Moreover, the computer affords the artists a new found pleasure through these engagements, inspiring a particular model of a hybrid maker. Working from a specific, yet partial perspective that Haraway names "situated knowledge," a new embodiment of the nonhuman computer within the organic body, calls for the artist to recognize their own semiotic technologies for making meaning. These semiotic technologies lie outside old and relativistic scientific narratives (pp. 188-190). The artists take responsibility for re-inscribing their bodies upon the digital spaces of making, and confirming their kinship with machines and the visual representations they facilitate.

Near the end of the cyborg manifesto essay, Haraway opens up the opportunity to continue the exploration of cyborgs by asking "Why should our bodies end at the skin?"(p.178). She offers up the cyborg as a new way of being and self making that cannot be dismissed. The cyborg is here, now. It represents a contemporary fractured subject that negotiates a myriad of networks by "both building and destroying machines, identities, categories, relationships, space stories" (p.181). The cyborg is more than an extension of human capacities. It is an incorporation of the computer/digital with the organic.

**New hybrids: Incorporating the cyborg with the artist**

When artists like Peter, Donna and Claire develop imagery using their home computers, their organic fingers *click,* or pulse the electronically connected computer mouse, directing the development of their designs. Their hands and bodies are not abandoned, but rather, they are mapped onto a network of digital gestures that connect to form their digitally mastered visual representations. "Mastering," however, is a contentious term and calls up notions of domination, a condition that the cyborg entity refuses. Perhaps, the computer work of the artists is better named as a *digital realization.*

Morse further pursues the proliferation of human-non-human kinships. She theorizes on other ways humans and machines can connect, yet still eradicate the myths of domination by rethinking this relationship. She suggests that one particular scenario sees the organic body as incorporated with the computer body. She claims that "the organic body cannot be abandoned, it might be fused with electronic culture in what amounts to an oral logic of *incorporation*" (1994:158). The computer ingests the artist, and the artist ingests the computer into their ways of working in more of an inside/outside dialectic. The logic of oral incorporation is a metaphorical "eating" through a mixing of bodies where one body is surrounded (eaten) by the other through introjection and absorption (p. 160). When the boundaries between one body and another (whether machine or human) are blurred, new forms of identity and subjectivity might fortify the self. According to Morse, this is how cyborgs eat. Therefore, the artist/maker must re-map organic qualities such as touch-space onto new virtual spaces in an embodied way as a condition of feeding the cyborg. The electronic skin of the computer screen and mouse becomes the conduit for engaging with the cyborg realm in these spaces. Sensory or haptical engagements are translated and remapped onto visual forms (*cf.* Lant 1995:68) and the visual encounter becomes the guiding principle for handwork. Again, Peter claims the computer offers him "a certain kind of control and quality . . . more so than I can do with my hand." He acknowledges that while not the same as his physical drawing with graphite, there is "a definite interaction going on" between himself and the computer in a combined effort to produce images.

Handwork in the cyborg realm is a triangulated kinship of body, mind, and machine. Heidegger's *thinking hand* is reclaimed as mediator of both the world of physical things through touch, and the digital world of pixilated images through the electronic skin of the computer mouse. This occurs in synchronicity with the image on the screen and the image in the artists' mind. The artists are charged with the new task of finding their relatedness to the physical world through the incorporation of their organic bodies with the electronic appendage of the computer mouse. This is not easy as Peter suggests. Working via the computer presents a kind of "remoteness" that both "fascinates and frustrates" him. The image glows at him in a way that presents his black shapes with a power he has not achieved before, yet he can't touch this image like he can his graphite drawings. He is still looking for something that connects him to his digital works in a tactile way.

Donna says that even though using a computer to manipulate and re-view her already created images extends her imagination in new ways, she still has "the sensation of being distanced from the work" which she remedies by printing the digital images and then adding her own handmade marks on top. The artists' need to rethink their ways of using a computer to include the hand movements driving the computer mouse albeit, they are different movements. That being said, Robyn claims the computer mouse is just another tool she uses for art making like a pencil or a paintbrush. She says "I think that they feel that they are different, but I don't think that they really are different." Robyn moves quite easily in the cyborg realm.

Haraway (1991) claims that the cyborg has no single origin nor distinct boundaries to envelop this new realm. How then do individuals, in particular the artists whose stories are included in this thesis, distinguish themselves from machines? How are they learning to reconstruct themselves through these electronic networks? Sofoulis, a former graduate student of Haraway's, calls our attention to new responsibilities inherent in acting within the cyborg realm. She interprets Haraway as more concerned with "the specificity of hybrid forms that arise in particular situations" than hybridity for its own sake (2001:17). Responsibility lies in maintaining a sense of movement across and in-between humans and machines in ways that contest "the mere grafting of two connecting points" (Haraway 1991 cited in Sofoulis 2001:16). Responsibility also lies in recognizing a new ethical position relative to commingling with technology, acknowledging the political and economic frameworks that underline the cyborg's evolution. Some of these structures involve a patriarchal dominance that the artists recognize in the form of the electronic Other and its prevailing presence in their new ways of art making. Sofoulis asks to what extent does the prevailing world view reorganize, celebrate, or, on the contrary, deny these particular hybridities? (p.17) The new hybrid cyborg art maker must be responsible for a more critically insightful engagement with technology, not merely using hybridity and the cyborg as a trend.

The machine, according to Haraway, does not exist to dominate or be dominated. Rather, the machine *is* us (p.180). The cyborg denounces the manual/digital dualism and reconsiders the relationship instead as a kinship actualized through co-opting and cooperation amongst diverse networks. The cyborg realm stimulates a disassembling and reassembling of human/nonhuman relationships, particularly those that involve human/machine interfaces. The cyborg is not afraid of joint kinships with machines. The cyborg privileges partial bodies and identities, contestations, deconstructions and contradictory standpoints, all of which are positions and strategies the postmodern artist assumes at varying times during the process of developing visual representations.

Jin considers himself a postmodern artist in part by the way he ingests information about the world around him through his computer and the Internet and then translates what he perceives through images produced by his own hand markings. Jin believes his hand to be "spiritual" a conduit of his soul which is a virtual presentation of self, yet not in a digital sense. The impetus for Jin's hand work is both digitally and soulfully virtual. He also claims that his art comes from his hand via "markings and drawing" but it is based on preliminary digital works of "pattern making and manipulating ideas." As much as Jin insists we all must become digital as a way of informing ourselves about the world, he also calls his application of physical art media to paper "old fashioned."

### Reading the artists' computer-based engagements through a Cyborg lens

Through the incorporation of home computers and digital graphic programs into otherwise manual hand making processes, artists are experiencing new relationships between themselves and electronic machines. The haptic touch-space so highly regarded by traditional artists engaged in hand making, is incorporated with new forms of encounters that offer possibilities for refashioning the capabilities of the artists' hands in ways that create new spatial relationships between their bodies, machines, and resulting images. The touch-space is reconstituted via the pulsing "click" of the computer mouse and a dependency on the eye and the screen for guidance. The eye, however, is not the only perspective necessary here. The cyborg's double vision is a result of the interdependent vision of the eye and the pixilated image on the screen, in an exchange of human and nonhuman perspectives. In this case, the resulting work is no longer from the single fixed position of the artist as it includes the digital visions of the computer and programmer. It is perhaps the second vision or perspective that the study artists experience as an electronic Other.

Donna remarks that the computer manipulations modify images she has already created in ways that, for her, change the meaning. She is prompted to think of her images from different perspectives. Yet, how does this double vision that is emerging from the joint kinship of artist and computer affect their perception of making? Has it prompted a new epistemology and a rethinking of art practice? Are the artists developing a new language to describe their ways of making that incorporates a computer? By rereading the artists' stories through a cyborg lens, I endeavour to answer these questions.

To begin, I would like to revisit Donna's comment that the interview questions I posed to her tended to blur the boundaries of the different aspects of computer use. She prefers to keep each function distinct, and named as such. For example, email, the Internet, graphics programs, and word processing, are all different and separate operations and she is right in part. It is interesting however, that the specific siting of Donna's computer, her bedroom which is an intimately domestic space, did not surface during our discussion of the role of the computer within her living and working life. The site specificity of the artists' computers is important "because it focuses attention" on the ways in which new media forms "blend with the social conventions and power structures of its locale" (McCarthy

2001: 2). Like the family television set, the computer not only adapts to the conventional spatial or sensorial arrangements of its location, "but it also enters into, and takes up a position within the immaterial networks of power that characterize family [or the artist's] life" (p.2). The specificity of location illustrates the particular spatial complexity of the media form (p.3). The ways in which Donna and the other artists locate their computers apart from their studios, denote their particular desire to maintain a boundary between the two forms of practice, and limiting the scale, or spatial discrepancy on which these forms are privileged in the artists' ways of producing images.

The particular placement of Donna's computer blurs the boundaries between the computer as a tool that provides distinct functions, and a domestic appliance that services needs (such as looking up medical information on the Web) and provides pleasure in varying degrees. While the bedroom may be the only physical space in the house to place the computer, Donna has allowed this electronic box (as many of us have) to impose itself on this intimate space and insinuate itself into her daily routines and rhythms. Perhaps we all tread within the cyborg realm already, to some degree.

Moreover, the computer is, in part, a conduit for communication through email, consumerism of data as well as material goods through the Web, a site of production of information, imagery, and refashioned, multiplicitous identities. While admittedly there are distinct functions, they all exist through the interweaving of networks that are re-woven into the various routines of Donna's daily life, all of which begin from her bedroom. While Donna's routines and daily workings incorporate the computer at different intervals, she seems to resist the ways in which the boundaries between her physical and computer-based encounters overlap, rendering their borders somewhat murky. In this way, Donna appears to contest the cyborg, preferring established dualisms to remain intact. That being said however, she breaks through those dualisms from time to time when she entertains new perspectives on her work that are facilitated by computer manipulations of her images. Donna is also very computer savvy, maintaining a Web design business that involves creativity spawned by her manual art practice and her more recently developed digital manipulation abilities. Donna's movements in between physical and virtual world routines illustrate this cyborg realm as a paradoxical space that often goes unnamed.

Peter mentions several times that he and other mid-career to senior artists he knows have/had "a foot in two camps" in relation to using the computer for making art and images. Peter claims that he relates best to static images and does not know how he fits into the dynamic imagery that is based in much of computer culture. He does not look upon his relation to digital image making as a kinship yet, even though he talks about the fragmentation of being both in the physical world of "making art," and the dynamic world instigated by the computer. Like Donna, he still perceives borders and boundaries between the two worlds even though he is working to break through those boundaries and more comfortably incorporate the machine into his processes.

The boundaries that are proliferating because of resistance to acknowledging the collaboration and kinship that artists are developing are further reinforced by the domestic positioning of their computers away from the sanctity of their studios. This site specificity calls into question larger assumptions about the role of the computer in the artists' living and working lives. The computer services specific needs as distinguished by Donna's compartmentalization of the various functions. By using the computer as a tool to service particular requirements, the artists are subordinating its role, and enhancing their own position within the creative process. This helps to retain a singular vision that of the human maker or *Homofaber*.

Artists such as Claire, Jack and Donna work to retain their autonomy as makers because of this monocular perspective on how they come to represent the world around themselves. They are resisting disruptions to fixed patterns of practice, or what Hayles (1993) describes as an intrusion of randomness. Her point is that bodies, like books, have a set pattern and content that are not easily changed or rewritten. This is also the case of static images and art works. Information technologies such as computers and computer programs are very easily changed, embracing randomness as a form of dynamic interaction with content, rewriting its encoding and meaning. The human body, the book, the durable materials that are artworks and static images, both transmit and store information within fixed centralized patterns. The interface between humans and computers is apparently complicated by randomness, described by Hayles (1993) as an absence of pattern, that contests fixed patterns and renders the content continually changeable and re-writeable. It is this particular concept that has the contingency of disrupting the artists' perception of what making images represents. The introjection of "randomness" is useful for considering the possibility of *double vision.* That being said, the artists do not yet have the vocabulary to name this double vision other than to describe another presence during their computer engagements.

**Double vision**

The presence of the electronic Other is sideswiped, however, when the artists subordinate the computer as a domestic tool instead of incorporating its nonhuman perspective within their studio practice. Peter says "I'm not sure we've found the voice of computer technology," when he relates how he is trying to refashion what he is doing in the physical world through digital manipulation. He has yet to find a vocabulary for describing the new relationships that are possible between him and his computer. Although he hints at the possibility of a double vision when he describes how the computer changes the scale on which he can view his work, providing new perspectives and possibilities he had not had the opportunity to consider otherwise. He has, nevertheless, yet to name this new form of envisioning.

Donna on the other hand, while contesting her archeological background, has endeavoured to categorize computer functions in the same colonizing fashion, resisting partial identities of artist, digital being, and entrepreneur. Donna denies the computer's spatiality within her making processes and defaults to her incessant need for the touch-space to be present in her hand making. Donna's resistance to blurring the boundaries may be preventing her from developing a vocabulary to describe her cyborg experiences, even though she delights in the new image capabilities she assumes through her collaborations with her computer. Donna has allowed the computer's manipulations of her work to become a new vision that affects her own perspective, not only of the new digital images, but in how the "real" physical works compare to the pixilized transmissions on the computer screen. For Donna, this is a form of double vision enabled by the computer/machine, but one she cannot name. The double vision prompted by new computerized perspectives, revisits questions that surfaced in relation to Elkins' concerns of superimposing modernist ideal methods of constructing visual imagery onto computer impressions, particularly when a new descriptive vocabulary is lacking.

Consideration of a kinship with her computer would disrupt Donna's assumptions about herself as an artist, which she has already described as a fragile perception. In light of the disruption of autonomous perspectives, Peter suggests that "what is not obvious, are exactly what common denominators are the tools of your [their] expression?" This intriguing question has implications beyond the superficial analysis of medium, subject, content, or presentation of imagery. Peter's question opens up the possibility of interrogating the ways in which artists develop their practice of producing images. Are they refashioning or adapting the workings of their practices in ways that speak to changes in the cultural, political, economic and technological environments, or are they commentating from the sidelines?

I think here again of Claire's comment that she is "intrigued by computer-based work a little bit, almost like somebody's intrigued by an accident." Claire's comment places her very much on the periphery of what is happening in digital culture, even though she is using her computer in ways that are informing her other work. She also keeps her computer in a space different from her art making studio because she says "the energies they require from me are conflicting. The computer takes me over in a different way . . . a kind of consuming where the studio fills me. It is where the real nourishment is." This consumption Claire describes is akin to Morse's theory of incorporation where one entity, the body, is enveloped by another, the machine (1995:158). Claire is consumed by the computer in a way that conflicts with her perspectives of what art making does for her physically. The conflicting, or contradictory standpoint, is characteristic of the cyborg realm, no matter how discomforting it may be. Claire, like Peter and Donna, resist these partial ways of being. They resist the incorporations of humans and non humans, even though the cyborg is increasingly, as Haraway (1991) points out, becoming their ontology.

Ironically, artists including myself and those named in this study, continuously proclaim that our role in society, as Claire suggests, is to encourage others to see things, sometimes ordinary things, "in a different way" beyond singular perspectives. Two of the younger artists, Robyn and Jin, both acknowledge the incorporation of the digital world into their ways of living and working. While they are also lacking a new vocabulary to describe the cyborg ontology, they do not resist engagements with the cyborg realm, or deny its pervasiveness. They have grown up with multiplicity in ways that enable to move from "real" to virtual worlds quite comfortably (Turkle 1995, Lanham 1993, Tapscott 1998). They have developed a visual aesthetics that includes digitized and pixilated imagery from video and computer-based games. The issue at hand, however, is the need for a vocabulary to describe their forms of making within the cyborg realm that includes engagements that are painful and pleasurable, as well as those that contest established assumptions about being an artist and art making practice.

**A cyborg vocabulary for artists**

What might a cyborg vocabulary for artists look like? I am speaking here of a vocabulary that would enable artists whose practices are primarily predicated on hand making to negotiate the digital world of developing images via a computer mouse and screen in a "symbiotic union between human and intelligent machine" (Hayles 1993: 5). In order to answer this question and begin to develop such a vocabulary, the artists involved must consider a position of resistance toward existing dualisms, dichotomies, and traditional meta-narratives regarding technology, the body and the act of making. They must not consider the computer as merely a "tool," an extension of the hand, "apart from the body that can be picked up and put down at will" (Hayles 1993), but rather as a co-maker of images that enacts a new spatial relationship, a "space of flows" that emphasizes interactivity and a fluid network of exchanges" (Castells 1996:398). These exchanges are most often experienced by electronic pulses, and the flows that occur between human organisms and information circuits through which work is processed. Castells' theory recognizes that our society "is constructed around flows: flows of capital, flows of information, flows of technology, flows of organizational interaction, flows of images, sounds and symbols" (p. 412). He claims that these flows are "an expression" of the dominating processes we live by (p. 412). Castells' concept is useful for reconsidering the connection between work that is crafted by hand in the studio, or developed using computer programs.

This position of resistance is inherently risky as it requires the artists to break down barriers and challenge assumptions about art making that, as Suzi Gablik suggests in her 1991 book, *The Reenchantment of Art*, can disrupt their assumptions about art making as a subjective individualistic exercise. In this way she explains, change will not occur "without consequences to the way we see and do things, and the uprooting of accustomed habits of thinking often has uncomfortable personal consequences" (p.8). Gablik further suggests that "the most fruitful developments are likely to take place where opposing lines of thought meet" (p.9).

Adopting a position of resistance also invokes a new technology of the self, refashioning the Foucauldian concept into what Miller terms *différends de soi* (1993:176). Foucault claims that technologies of the self grant individuals "operations on their bodies and souls, thoughts, conduct, and a way of being, so as to transform themselves in order to attain a certain state of happiness, purity, wisdom, perfection, or immortality" (1983:18). It is a "private search for autonomy" (Miller 1993:176). Miller suggests however that technologies of the self are conflated between this yearning for autonomy "unfettered by institutionally imposed powers" and a freedom of speech "that is granted by the public space that democracy alone can offer" (p.178). Therefore, *différends de soi,* represents the "feasibility of autoinvention" (178). Miller borrows Lyotard's definition of *the différend* to mean "an unstable condition, a moment in language when something that must be put into words cannot yet be" (Miller 1993:180; *cf.* Lyotard 1983:29).

*Différends de soi*, invokes the pluralized self that enables an individual to make their own life, "beyond the alienation that is produced by defining the self in terms of the prevailing mode of governance" and the social and cultural codes that dominate (Miller 1993: 207). In postmodernity, this at the very best, says Miller, can spawn "an overtly pluralized cultural self" (p. 208) in ways that construct identity beyond what is already being offered (pp. 208 & 223). This pluralized self transcends dualisms and embraces contradictory standpoints. Assuming the cyborg as one of those pluralisms opens up "the possibility of fashioning ourselves anew in a distinctive postmodern way," a form that Miller claims "transcend the opposites of beauty and ugliness"(p.208). This refashioning must incorporate the body in such a way as it is not lost in Cartesian separations of mind from body, or the body's severance from all machine-based workings.

Claire appears to be dealing with a new pluralized self while working both manually and on or "in" her computer. She talks about being physically drawn in by both the manipulative capabilities of the computer and the immersive condition prompted by her hand drawing procedures. She acknowledges that there is a distinction between the two, but cannot name the physicality of working by computer. This is *the différend* at work. She names the physical process of working by hand as "Flow" but cannot yet put words to the physical feeling of being "in the computer." Perhaps this is because "being in the computer" is a virtual concept of self that is different from the virtuality of her "soulful" self. They are both virtual, but they are also different in that one is near in the haptical sense and one is far in an optical sense.

Miller (1993), Haraway (1991), and Hayles (1993), all use the term *coupling* or *couplet* to name relationships that appear to be contradictory. Haraway, suggests that imagining the cyborg has the potential to produce "fruitful couplings" of human and nonhuman (1991:151) relationships. Miller explains the manufacturing of *différends de soi*, for example in how "the sacred and the profane are rendered as a couplet" or an interdependence of two seemingly opposite ideas (1993:207). Hayles uses coupling to imply an "intense and multifaceted" union of "biological organism and the information circuits in which it is enmeshed" (1993: 5). Thus, coupling may be a useful term as part of a cyborg vocabulary for artists. The term implies interdependency between two entities that create some new form of energy.

A particularly interesting definition of *coupling* offered by *Webster's Universal College Dictionary* (1997) is "the association of two circuits or systems in such a way that power may be transferred from one to the other." I propose that the artists' way of naming their computer engagements be considered as this kind of *coupling*. The artist and machine are coupled in ways that join organic sensing bodies with the information and communication conduits of the computer, in the pursuit of producing energies that result in the development of visual images and works of art. The conjoined energies of organism and machine continue to be manifested in marks, gestures, bits, bytes and pixels interdependent of each other.

Power is relayed from the organic to the digital and also from the digital to the organic. Each side of the coupling takes its turn at devouring the other. This coupling is based within the network of interweaving circuits of meaning and making, embodied in the work of the artist.

The new cyborg inspired vocabulary for artists is not predicated on ideal methods of image production that are grounded in modernist narratives, nor does it superimpose a dependence on physical properties and the language to describe these properties onto digital transmissions. The cyborg vocabulary employs an imagination based on couplets of organic bodies and digital circuits that interweave through spatial flows of image, text, bodies, and bytes.

In the same way that the term "coupling" is useful for describing human/computer collaborative workings, the touch-space of hand-working is refashioned through Castells' concept "space of flows." Touch-space is interchanged with a flow of information and imagery through electronic circuits and pulses. This exchange inspires new couplings of embodied imaginings and digital image development. One form of space does not negate the other but rather enters into "the material organization of time-sharing" that the artists' ways of working "flow through" (Castells 1996: 412). The artist embodies a new pluralized "self as an auto invention," unencumbered by dominant codes of the past (Miller 1993: 219). This pluralized self moves through the cyborg realm, not always comfortably, but in ways that begin to initiate new couplings of human and machine workings in an effort to produce images and make art.

### Establishing a comfort level within the cyborg realm

Feenberg suggests that there "has been a long-standing humanist distrust of computers." The computer "appears as the very emblem of the modern experiment in total rational control" (2002:117). The human-machine relationship has become more contentious as new media configurations incorporate themselves into ways of working and living in postmodernity. However, new forms of human/machine complementarities are emerging, thereby increasing the opportunities for greater technological choice (Zuboff cited in Feenberg 2002). This complementarity is based on a cooperative venture that exploits human capabilities of "dealing with unexpected situations and responding to novelty" with computer abilities to "organize the vast amount of data required for modern production" (p. 123). It is an exchange between directing unpredictability, and managing information in the effort to produce images and art works.

That said however, the body still figures prominently in the way choices are made and the ways in which the artists use computer technologies. Boler (2003) contends that even when individuals are engaged in the multiplicitous world of cyberspace, they have a deep need to retain some connection to the physical body, both their own and the physical bodies of others they encounter as the final determination of an authentic truth that informs meaning. If particular artists are to resist participating in developing and engaging new vocabularies that describe the discursive spaces of hand making and computer generated collaborations in which they already partake, they are as Foucault (1971) suggests, disempowering themselves at the very limits of their disciplines.

Emphasizing the importance of choice in the development of new couplings by artists incorporating their home computers within their primarily handmade art production empowers them to participate in a cyborg realm that they can name. As well, artists making work by hand have the opportunity to experience a new range of potentialities in the cyborg realm through the possibilities facilitated by double vision, a coupling of both human and computer perspectives of the world. As Feenberg contends, these potentialities are defined as occurring through "aesthetic experimentation, ethical and political debate, and technical controversies" (2002:128). Artists who adopt and accept the potentialities of double vision will gain a comfortable understanding of their physical presence as artists within digital and virtual cultures.

The next chapter addresses the implications of the study findings and my research on the cyborg realm, in particular the importance of developing new vocabularies for art making processes that couple hand making and computer manipulating procedures for producing images. The implications are examined in relation to both artists' professional practices and the area of art education that focuses on the "teaching studio." I also discuss how this whole investigative process, which appeared as an aporia for me at the start, has affected the ways in which I perceive my own art making practice. It is a discussion that is intended to open up questions for other artists about their own engagements with computers.

# CHAPTER SEVEN: IMPLICATIONS FOR ARTISTS AND ART EDUCATORS

## Key issues at stake

Theoretical discourses and phenomenological data have facilitated my exploration into the ways in which artists are using their personal computers to assist and sometimes replace their hand making procedures. In particular, I have reported on the ways in which six specific artists are integrating computers into their art making practices through a qualitative analysis of experiences they described in face-to-face interviews. The primary objective of this research study was to shed light on the challenges and accomplishments, terms of resistance and incorporation that earmark the relations of interchanging hand and computer procedures of image production and art making. My intent from the beginning has been to extract salient issues from the artists' stories that could be further explored in relation to changes in cultural production, specifically two-dimensional image making within an evolving digitized and globalized environment.

Three major themes and five sub-themes were threaded throughout the artists' conversations and relevant to my initial questions of how artists are using computers within their art making practices. From these themes however, two particular issues I had not anticipated when I began this research project surfaced. The first of these issues is concerned with the reconstitution of haptical space when making art by computer and the second issue is concerned with the emergence of *the cyborg* within the artists' making practices. A significant implication of artists negotiating the cyborg realm is the impact of *coupling* and its potential for opening up a new vocabulary for describing processes of working concurrently in both physical and virtual environments. Without considering new concepts such as coupling, the displacements attributed to computer technologies and the digitization of image production tend to separate *the hand* from *the machine*. This separation reinforces the perception that art making by hand and machine are two very disparate ways of producing images. Instead of bypassing significant connections, it is time to address the ways in which alliances between the two can be reconstituted and studied in relation to both established artists' practices and the teaching studios employed in art education. These new connections are both beneficial and pleasurable.

The six artists interviewed for the micro study part of this research remarked that while they incorporate a variety of computer applications in their making processes, they had not considered questions about their relationship to making in conjunction with a machine. They had not addressed their own kinships with different forms of computerized systems that had been facilitating particular aspects of their handmade creative processes. Their own absorption with the hands-on production and their immersion in the haptic spaces produced by their creative processes often subverted any in-depth analysis of how they were accommodating the computer and how the computer was facilitating an extension of their hand-making abilities. In light of this perceived act of avoidance, all practicing artists might reconsider the ways they are constructing and asking questions about the world through the work they are producing by hand and machine. Digital technology has prompted artists to experiment with new ways to revisit old questions while at the same time consider new questions as they emerge. I maintain that the way artists are recoding meaning through their work is in direct relation to the ways they adopt particular cultural practices, including those engaging new technologies.

This concluding chapter addresses the broader implications of my research and the coupled relationship between artists and computers. Issues that have surfaced in relation to the new kinships formed are immediately relevant to the field of art education, the teaching of art making, and the self-imposed studio pedagogy of both emergent and established artists working in the current digital culture. The immediate task of developing a vocabulary for describing these coupled kinships and relationships is integral to understanding new forms of image production and art making practice.

**Shifts in dominant, residual and emergent categories of cultural production and art making practice**

The autonomous artist is "manifested in a specific set of relations that is directly linked with the nature of their immediate means of production" (Williams 1981:112). The artist who hand makes work is often under the assumption they have autonomy over the thing they are making, taking pleasure in their immediate relationship with their materials, their physical processes and their "creation." Although, as I have already stated, the artists are not autonomous creators, they are cultural producers within the changing dynamics of social processes. The artists' stories included in my research describe the ways in which they hold onto tradition while at the same time, experiment with innovative new media. *Tradition*, Williams explains, is a self-evident process of "deliberate continuity . . . a selection and reselection of those significant received and recovered elements of the past which represent not a necessary, but desired community" (p.187). What happens then, when artists begin to incorporate machines such as computers that have active programs and processes designed by other individuals in less than familiar communities? Instead of existing as individual producers within desired communities, artists become involved in new forms of group production and are introduced to communities outside their traditional selections. The group production spawns "a range of developing relationships, many directly related to changes in the means of production" which, in the case of artists working with computers translates to a new division of labour (p.113). The computer programs exchange some of the laborious tasks of hand rendering for *slick* and efficient manipulations achieved through the click of the computer mouse. The computer also helps "manage" the means of production through these efficient procedures in ways that render the artists distanced from the work (p. 113). The computer mediates the tasks of the artists often offering multiple options.

Williams delineates *the dominant*, *the residual*, and *the emergent* as three interrelated conditions for analyzing the dynamic relations of social and cultural change in regards to cultural production. The artists described in the research study can be mapped across these three distinctions at different points in their stories. These distinctions are apparent in the ways they negotiate between physical and virtual worlds through a variety of hegemonic, counter hegemonic and alternative positions. The *dominant* positions the artists take are "to a presumed (and then dominant) autonomy of professional and aesthetic values" (p. 204). They may not be fully aware of this form of control. Many times the artists implied their need for this autonomy. They sought out the pleasure of physically "creating" by hand. This perspective is affected by the social and economic constructions of the dominant art world and its market for "original" art objects. It is also symptomatic of the "capitalist" art world's prescription for artists to be creative masters within our culture.

The *residual* is evident as "work made in earlier and often different societies and times, yet still available and significant" (Williams 1981:204). Some of the six artists interviewed spoke "romantically" about the "spiritual" pleasures of creating art objects and images. This sensibility is the residue of past thinking based on modernist conceptions of art making that resurface throughout several of their stories. In contrast, the *emergent* is "work of various new kinds" (p.204). The emergent invites innovation, yet not to the point where it completely topples the dominant. The dominant can "absorb or attempt to absorb" both residual and emergent distinctions of cultural production. However, there are almost always groups and communities that keep "available" older forms just as "there is almost always new work which tries to move (and at times succeeds in moving) beyond the dominant forms" (p.204) as the three are always in play with each other.

The artists' stories illustrate the play between these distinct conditions of cultural production as they describe how they negotiate new terrains, particularly that of the cyborg. The dominant condition of the artists' autonomy is challenged by the pluralized self that is inherent in the emergent cyborg ways of working. Yet, the residual modernist is kept "available" as the artists move from the computer back to hand making in an effort to retain a hapticity that is reminiscent of older forms of production. The emergent, says Williams, "is related to but not identical to the innovatory" (p.205). It does not completely destroy *the dominant* in ways persistent and disturbing innovations might. Rather the emergent and the dominant create a complex tension to which there may be no resolution. The cyborg realm embraces this complex tension quite readily.

**Implications of the cyborg realm on established art making practices**

Producing images within the conceptual space of the cyborg realm requires artists to rethink the effects of cultural change across both physical and virtual worlds. Their means of art production are often affected by changes that can occur both immediately yet at the same time, also take an extended period to develop their full potential. The Web, for instance, is forcing cultural change (Lovejoy 1997:213). It has inspired new possibilities for interaction, collaboration, exhibition, and creation which are transforming production and dissemination opportunities not only for established artists, but students too. The Web is already used by some artists as an opportunity to collaborate on different works, collapsing physical distances, coming together in "special composite image spaces" where they can "mix spaces or exchange spaces in a new kind of collage" (Lovejoy 1997:218).

Many artists who are new to computer technology and cyberspace are not always comfortable connecting and collaborating in virtual spaces. They use the Web as an electronic library for research and concept development yet refer back to anachronistic processes and residual perceptions of traditional library communities. This raises concerns of how artists are finding a comfortable position in cyber-culture and exploring the Web as a medium that can shape their art making practices. A particular implication of the Web on art practices is the way artists are learning to mediate excess information through a process of editing and selecting salient bits and then integrating their new knowledge with their established anachronistic modes of image production, repurposing those modes in the process (*c.f.* Collins 1995). Employing the Web as a form of global research library calls for a new type of pedagogy within art making studios that enables artists to see the role of information producing technologies as socially constructed entities with their own forms of meta narratives prescribed by a dominant digital culture.

Garoian and Gaudelius identify a "cyborg pedagogy" which produces a conceptual space for critiquing the interrelatedness of the body and technology. They offer cyborg pedagogy as serving "a complex metaphor that represents the body/technology hybrid, while it exposes the cyborg's dialectical pedagogy of inscription and resistance" (2001:334). Garoian and Gaudelius define inscription as "the world's imposition on the body" (p.337). Cyborg pedagogies can be used to critique the ways in which artists transfer social perceptions and practices onto their technological interactions and draw meaning from those engagements (p.346). These are important considerations for those artists who are suspect of the controlling structures of an electronic Other whether on the Web or through commercial graphics programs such as *Photoshop*. Cyborg pedagogies provide a way to ask questions about limitations and controlling variables imposed by dominant narratives and provide new ways of thinking about the implications of image production in a digital culture. Cyborg pedagogies also offer artists opportunities to critique the different inscriptions of digital technologies on themselves, and resist hegemonic precepts in exchange for developing pleasurable relationships with technologies on their own terms.

As artists develop forms of cyborg pedagogy they open up the possibility of disrupting the meta narratives imposed by the dominant culture's prescribed role of technology on their lives and art practices. They have the occasion to facilitate a critical reading of their engagements with information technologies exposing oppressive and controlling tactics that come to bear on the meanings they are creating, as well as develop new human/machine kinships that are pleasurable. Cyborg pedagogies "challenge the assumptions of information technologies as shaped by the dominant culture" and "explores the varied means that artists, educators, and cultural theorists use to expose, critique, and intervene in the ways that technology is conceived" (Garoian & Gaudelius, 2001, p.346). To this end, cyborg pedagogy offers the opportunity for more informed negotiations of the cyborg realm, critically positioning artists so they may imagine new forms of image production based on their own perspectives and constructions of human/machine couplings. Cyborg pedagogy is also implicated in the ways artists name and describe these couplings as a form of cyborg vocabulary.

## Developing new forms of digital hapticity

A particular by-product of the new forms of image production I have been describing in the cyborg realm is the reconstitution of haptical space. The hapticity of the computer screen is a space that is predicated on the physical effect of viewing images that as Peter claims, "glow." In order to flesh out the implications of this new hapticity I am borrowing here Collins' arguments for reconstituting some form of an aura in relation to reproduced cultural products. I am refashioning some of his salient points and modifying them for my own arguments for a digital hapticity in relation to computer screens.

Collins contends that Benjamin's theories regarding the aura are tied only to presence and to bearing witness within a specific tradition. They do not account for personal projections of value onto an object which are intertwined with social, political, cultural, and economic factors (p. 23). Collins maintains that "the nature and function of aura changes as it becomes variable according to location" (p. 24).

The postmodern project has released the fixed location of cultural objects in ways that pluralize meaning. In order to examine art and culture in the age of digital reproduction, critics and users alike must begin from a premise that is not dependent upon bearing witness to an original, but rather start from a position of understanding the proliferation of the aura "as it has been dispersed through the multiplication of information technologies" (p. 25). In other words, artists and viewers alike must re-inscribe their own personal investments onto images that are created using reproductive technologies such as the computer, in ways that take into account the diversification of meaning that is inherent in image proliferation and manifested through personal investments.

That being said, the touch-space related to physical objects also becomes dispersed across personal investments in the computer screen images that are dependent on an optical objectivism (Lant 1995). The personal investments induce a physical experience within the individual through particular meanings invoked by an image and the "shock" of its presentation. For example, the "glow" of the image proliferates via dynamic media such as the web or complex computer graphics programs in contrast to the static presence of a painting. The combination of meanings projected by the individual and their experience of the image "glowing" back at them has the potential to prompt a sensation that is perceived as physical. Peter asserts "there is some sort of interaction happening." All of the artists interviewed described this experience at various points in their accounts of viewing their own images on their computer screens. This new form of hapticity represents a shift in sense perceptions that readily affect the ways in which these particular artists experience their making processes. The issue of digital or computer screen hapticity merits greater attention and further study across larger populations of artists producing images using computers.

**Visual art and media education in the cyborg realm**

Moving art making practices into the cyborg realm has important implications for art education and for educators engaged in studio-based teaching and learning. Art education and art making are not easily separated from other disciplines that involve visual culture such as media studies. Buckingham (1990) suggests that educators of media studies and new textual forms are responsible for giving students "access to different discourses to new and hopefully productive ways of making sense of their own experiences with the media" (p. 216). In this same way, art educators must consider new forms of visual literacy that reconsider how visual ness is constructed and reproduced through various media forms and new couplings of human and machine efforts. This involves opening up the possibility of digital epistemologies that pose new ways of knowing about media and new forms of expertise. In addition, this may also involve drawing connections between what were once thought of as contradictory practices, for example handmade art production and computer reproduction.

Buckingham cites Bruner in calling for a conceptual way of learning that invokes in students a process of "recoding what they see and do" in ways that prompt "new modes of organization with the new products that have been formed by these recodings" (1990:221). Educators must encourage students to interrogate all the media forms they are using in ways that include their experiences across a wide range of disciplines and practices, not simply adopt the prescribed practices and assumptions of others (Buckingham 1990:223). This includes the ways in which media forms have been connected and related to one another, and the ways they have been kept separate.

Art education is notorious for cordoning off disciplines into distinct areas of practice and inquiry, reluctant to couple various relationships in new ways outside of the catchall arena of interdisciplinary studies. Working by hand and by computer may be a form of interdisciplinarity, but more importantly it is a coupling that needs acknowledging for its own sake because of its distinct ontological and epistemological implications for art making. There is also the issue of pleasure. Students, as Buckingham notes, must be given space to explore their "emotional investments in the media on their own terms . . . and give voice to their own pleasures" (p. 224).

The pleasures provoked by digital epistemologies that embrace the coupling of hand and computer procedures for making images suggest powerful linkages to innovation and imagination. These pleasures have more often been marginalized in formal educational situations in favour of learning formal applications of technique and what Elkins identified as ideal methods of image production. However, it is important to consider how teachers' own media experiences and pleasures affect how they guide their students (Morgan 1998:146-147). As demonstrated by the artists I interviewed, not all individuals engaging in image production are completely comfortable with computer integrations in art making practices. The *hand work* and *computer work* are sometimes segregated as the artists develop and produce images. This segregation could carry over into the classroom where kinships between students and computers are not openly recognized or celebrated.

The cyborg realm and cyborg pedagogies are implicated in reconstructive approaches to art education and the teaching studio. Clark calls for a reconstructed art education that is "designed to develop a sense of cultural relativity and cultural perspective among all students" prompting them "to compare their personal cultural values with contemporary and historical alternatives" (1996:80). This involves valuing art objects made by students "primarily for the meaning they convey, rather than for the formalist characteristics that they exhibit, and their ability to spark connections among related visual images" (p.80). The first step in this project however, is to recognize the art making activity of students as "cultural production" (Pearse 1992:250 cited in Clark 1996:80).

Educators adopting reconstructive approaches for studio-based teaching and learning can help students to negotiate the cyborg realm by encouraging them to think about the connections they make between making work by hand and incorporating computer produced images. Students can be encouraged to ask questions about how these connections affect the meanings they are creating in their work. Educators might pose questions to students about the ways they describe connections between images they produce by hand and images they produce by computer and how the different procedures affect their resulting works. How do the works produced by their coupling hand made and computer made images compare with works produced entirely by hand or entirely by computers? What are the benefits, limitations and pleasures of working by hand, or computer or through a kinship of both?

Duncum argues that a reconstructed art education exposes students to "an orientation toward the future" in ways "alternative possible futures are articulated" (Duncum 1991:54 cited in Clark 1996:81). Students working in the cyborg realm have the opportunity to articulate new possibilities that occur because of their kinship with computers as they develop into cultural producers on their own terms. Moreover, art educators should be cognizant of the implications of students straddling physical and virtual worlds while they learn to produce imagery, and make efforts to ensure they have vocabularies available to describe and articulate new ways of working by hand and computer. As part of such efforts, educators need to commit themselves to rethinking the ways in which art making is taught using traditional methods and the ways in which digital workings are incorporated into these forms of production. Educators must also reconsider the ways in which kinships with computers are affecting students' questioning of the world around them, paying close attention to the terms on which those questions are constructed.

## Gateways to furthering the research

The study I have described and discussed in this book is only a beginning. Further research that explores how young student artists are negotiating both physical and virtual worlds as they learn how to develop and produce images that contribute to cultural production is also needed. These new studies could examine how elementary students make connections between images they produce by hand and those they create using a computer, as well as exploring the implications of human/computer kinships on secondary and post secondary studio-based teaching and learning environments. Additional research that examines the impact of working by hand and computer on the educators themselves is also key to understanding the shifts in art making and art education brought about by digital technology. How are educators negotiating the cyborg realm within their own art practices and art classrooms?

Another area for further investigation I have already identified is the new form of computer screen hapticity that is developing as more visual artists move to the computer as a way of developing and producing imagery. This particular topic would revisit Benjamin's "Work of Art" essay in an effort to rethink the reproduction of images that are represented through the "glow of the screen." Investigations of this sort could explore the shifts in sense perceptions that are happening because of digital reproduction and how these shifts are impacting on both makers and viewers of "art" images.

Finally, an area that has aroused my interest as a result of this study and invites further investigation is the *performativity* employed by visual artists. This issue that I did not speak to involves artists performing *homo faber*, artists performing the cyborg, and artists performing in isolation and within communities. In her conversations, Donna alludes to her performativity when she describes "dancing with her paint brush" which she suggests would not happen with a computer mouse. She hints at a much larger area for investigation that involves new forms of hapticity and intimate proximity to machines. Butler says that acts or gestures of an individual "are performative in the sense that the essence or identity that they otherwise purport to express are *fabrications* manufactured and sustained through corporeal signs and other discursive means"

(1999:173). The performative "suggests a dramatic and contingent construction of meaning" (p.177). While some artists may contest that they are not performing acts *of being artists*, they *are* artists, performativity theory has interesting implications in regards to how acts of "making" may also be seen as forms of embodied performance. I foresee performativity theories as useful for investigating the ways in which artists *perform* across multiple domains that include physical and virtual territories. An investigation of this kind would contribute greatly to the scant amount of literature that addresses the ways in which artists work at *being artists*.

**Contemplations on my own art making practice**

As I mentioned at the beginning of this book, my research project is directly related to questions I had about my own art making practices. Before beginning this process, I viewed "the machine" as an intermediary in the development and production of my own image production. The manipulation of images enabled by the photocopier was, and still is stimulating and favorable. However, I did not consider this particular working arrangement a "kinship." My focus was directed on my apparent inability to return to the physical procedures of painting that I had once relied on. The aporia I experienced was the impassable point represented by the exchange of physical painting movement for the seduction of manipulative abilities via the machine. I found pleasure in my new kinship with the machine and with that pleasure some guilt. I felt that I should be able to return to painting, but something about the machine was creating the impasse. This is still an issue that to me feels unresolved. Yet my exploration of the cyborg realm has tempered what once appeared as an impassable juncture.

In the cyborg realm conflicts are often unresolved. Instead, the unresolvable are presented as a continuous tension that swells and subsides at various points in accordance with cultural change. New technologies are introduced to cultural practices. These technologies are then incorporated effecting more changes and fluctuations in the tension. Although as Gablik argues, it is at these tensest points in thought and production that "the most fruitful developments are likely to take place" (1991: 9). My new kinship with the photocopier has prompted me to work in ways that have been both beneficial and pleasurable. Listening to the artists' stories of their struggles and successes of making art by hand and computer, and exploring cyborg discourses through the work of authors like Haraway and Hayles has facilitated a qualitative change in the way I think about art practice. In particular, I have come to understand my own art making as a form of coupling and collaboration that exists within a particular tension between dominant, residual and emergent categories of production.

As cultural shifts increasingly affect the ways we all receive, interpret and make meaning from our experiences in the world, we are confronted with the need to transform old practices, sometimes working through difficult phases of translation. However, we must embrace these changes as necessary, beneficial and often pleasurable as we negotiate physical and virtual territories together. A better understanding of our kinships with computers will enable us to move more assuredly within the domain of the cyborg.

**Appendix A: Interview Questions**

1. Where do you get your ideas for making art?

2. What outside cultural, social, or technological factors influence you when you are exploring an idea for art making?

3. How do you research those ideas?

4. Have you always explored or researched in this way? If so, have you developed certain exploration rituals or practices that you follow more often than not? What forms do these practices take?

**OR** if your answer is no, what other ways of exploring or investigating ideas have you used?

5. How do you define the term exploratory practice?

6. Do you think you can use the investigative strategies for exploring an idea in one discipline or form of practice and apply it to another?

7. Do you use any exploratory strategies that you engage for art making for any other kind of investigating in your daily life?

8. How do you think the information age has affected the way you research and explore ideas?

9. How has it changed the ways in which artists work? Has it affected the physical art community?

10. Has continuous access to information over the Web affected the way you work, whether that be through researching, presenting, or creating?

11. Has the perceived collapse of time and space of the Internet affected traditional ways that artists work? Has it changed the ways in which traditional art making is valued, by artists, by society?

12. In your view, have digital technologies and the information age changed the way our culture reads images and understands a sense of aesthetics?

13. Has it changed the way artists read images? Has it changed the way you read digital images, analog images...read your own work?

14. How does a computer and digitized imagery affect the "haptic relationship" inherent in the way you work, i.e. your physical relationship to the screen vs. canvas, paper etc?

15. How well do you feel traditional art work is presented on the Web (yours or someone else's)? Does it change the way you think about presenting work? If it is your work, does seeing digital representations affect the way you approach your work or re-work ideas? How do you feel about being that accessible to others?

16. In regards to your own, general Web surfing practice, do you always have a predetermined idea or subject in mind when Web surfing or do you often log on and just wander? How do you choose which links you should follow to other web sites?

17. Web surfing is an exploratory practice in the sense that it involves the investigation of some form of subject matter or the probing of an idea. Do you

agree? Why or Why not? Do you research ideas for art making on the Web?

18. How does researching an idea by fleshing out possibilities and discovering trajectories using word search systems and following hyper-linked Web sites compare with the act of developing ideas in sketch books, on scraps of paper or even computer programs in order to produce images using traditional art media such as paint or pencil?

19. How would you define the aesthetic properties of the Web? Are there any common aesthetic principles at work for both traditional (analog) art and digital images found on the Web or are there divergent ones?

20. Do you keep a list of favourite web sites you can return to? What's on that list? How often do you return to it?

21. How has your knowledge of computers and exposure to the Internet and the Web changed the way you work now as opposed to before computers?

22. Have you, or would you ever consider giving up your traditional ways of working in order to completely digitize your processes? What would be the circumstances for this? How do you think it would affect your investigative and creative process?

23. How does a traditional artist redefine themselves in a digital culture?

24. What is your role as an artist in society?

25. Are you this same artist in cyberspace?

## Appendix B: Email Survey Questions

## Artist Profile Questionnaire

Thank you for your participation. The following questions are designed to help me develop a profile on you as a study participant. It will also help establish the study group demographics. You may simply insert your answers in point form if you wish after each question and send the completed survey as a reply to this email. As in the interview, your anonymity will be protected and you may opt out of answering any of the questions.

Thank you.

1. How old are you? (there are specific reasons for knowing the age range of participants as some theorists believe that computer and Internet use has generational differences. I hope to interview participants from a broad age range)
2. How long have you been an artist?
3. How did you come to know that you wanted to make art as part of your life's work?
4. Where do you make your work?
5. What kind of art do you make?
6. Have you always worked in this (these) formats and media, if not what else have you done?
7. How much time per day or week or month (whatever is applicable) do you spend making art?
8. Where do exhibit and/or present your work?
9. Do you use a computer daily? Approximately, on average, how much time do you spend each day (or week)?
10. For what purposes do you use a computer?
11. Where is your computer located?
12. How much of your computer time is spent using the Internet (or the Web)?

13. Do you have a dial-up or high speed connection?

14. Do you currently have a web site of your work, if not, has your work ever been presented over the Web at any point in time? Do you like how the work looks digitally presented?

**REFERENCES**

Arendt, H. (1998). *The human condition* (second edition). Chicago: The University of Chicago Press.

Aronowitz, S.& Menser, M. (1996). On cultural studies, science, and technology. In Aronowitz, S., Martinsons, B, & Menser, M. (Eds.), *Technoscience and cyberculture* (pp.7-27). New York: Routledge.

Barthes, R. (1977). *Image music text.* (S. Heath, Trans.). New York: Hill & Wang.

Barnard, M. (1998). *Art, design and visual culture.* New York: St. Martin's Press.

Barrett, T. (1994). *Criticizing art: Understanding the contemporary.* Mountain View, CA: Mayfield Publishing Company.

Batchen, G. (1998). Spectres of cyberspace. In N. Mirzoeff (Ed.), *The visual Culture reader* (pp. 273-278). New York: Routledge.

Baudrillard, J. (1983). *Simulations.* (P. Foss, P. Patton and P. Beitchman, Trans.). New York: Semiotext(e).

Becker, C. (1996). *Zones of contention.* Albany: State University of New York Press.

Becker, C. (2002). *Surpassing the spectacle.* New York: Rowman & Littlefield Publishers Inc.

Benjamin, W. (1968). *Illuminations.* H. Arendt (Ed.). ( H. Zohn, Trans.). New York: Schocken Books.

Blandy, D. & Congdon, K. (1987). *Art in a democracy.* New York: Teachers College Press.

Blumer, H. (1969). *Symbolic interactionism.* Berkely: University of California Press.

Boler, M. (2003).The New Digital Cartesianism: Bodies and Spaces in Online Education (forthcoming, *Philosophy of Education Society Yearbook,*)

Bolter, J. & Grusin, R. (2000). *Remediation: Understanding New Media.* Cambridge MA: The MIT Press.

Borsa, J. (1996). Nomadic Locations. In Walter Phillips Gallery Edition, *Naming a practice: Curatorial strategies for the future*. Banff: Banff Centre Press.

Bruckman, A. (1995). *Cyberspace is not Disneyland: The role of the artist in a networked world.* Retrieved 12/16/99 from: http://www.cc.gatech.edu/%7Easb/papers/getty/disneyland.html

Buckingham, D. (1990). Making it Explicit: Towards a theory of media learning. In D. Buckingham (Ed.), *Watching Media Learning* (pp.215-225). London: The Falmer Press .

Buck-Morss, S. (1992). Aesthetics and anaesthetics: Walter Benjamin's artwork essay reconsidered, *October* 62, 3-41.

Buck-Morss, S. (1995). The City as dreamworld and catastrophe, *October* 73 Summer, 3-26.

Burbules, N. (2000). Aporias, webs and passages: Doubt as an opportunity to learn. *Curriculum Inquiry*. 30(2) 171-188.

Butler, J. (1999). *Gender trouble*. New York: Routledge.

Casey, E. (1996). How to get from space to place in a fairly short stretch of time. In S. Feld & K. Basso (Eds.), *Senses of place* (pp.13-52). Santa Fe: School of American Research Press.

Castells, M. (1996). *Rise of the network society*, Vol. 1. London: Blackwell.

Csikszentmihalyi, M. (1990). *Flow, The psychology of optimal experience*. New York: Harper Collins Publishers.

Clark, R. (1996). *Art education: Issues in postmodernist pedagogy*. Reston: National Art Education Association.

Cohen, H. (1988). How to draw three people in a botanical garden. *Proceedings of the American Association for Artificial Intelligence,* 846-855.

Coldwell, P. (2001). *Interrogating the surface*. Unpublished paper, Chelsea:UK.

Collins, J. (1995). *Architectures of excess*. New York: Routledge.

Collins, J. & Mayblin, B. (2000). *Introducing Derrida* (second printing). Cambridge, UK: Icon Books Ltd.

Crary, J. (1999). *Techniques of the observer.* Cambridge, Mass: MIT Press (ninth edition).

Crary, J. (2000). *Suspensions of perception: Attention, spectacle, and modern culture.* Cambridge: MIT Press.

De Certeau, M. (1984). *The practice of everyday life.* Berkeley: The University of California.

De Kerckhove, D. (1995). *The skin of culture: investigating the new electronic reality.* Toronto: Somerville House Publishing

De Kerckhove, D. (1997). *Connected intelligence.* Toronto: Somerville House Publishing.

Deleuze, G. (1993). Music and Ritornello. In C. Boundas (Ed.), *The Deleuze Reader* (pp.201-203). New York: Columbia University Press.

De Lauretis, T. (1987). *Technologies of gender: Essays on theory, film and fiction.* London: Macmillan.

De Lillo, D. (1986). *White noise.* New York: Penguin Books.

Denzin, N. K., & Lincoln, Y. S. (1994). Introduction: Entering the field of qualitative research. In N. K. Denzin & Y. S. Lincoln (Eds.), *Handbook of qualitative research* (pp. 1-17). Newbury Park, CA: Sage

Derrida, J. (1987). Geschlecht II: Heidegger's hand. In J. Sallis (Ed.), *Deconstruction and Philosophy* (pp.161-196). Chicago: The University of Chicago Press.

Dienst, R. (1995). *Still life in real time: Theory after television.* Durham: Duke University press.

Dinkla, S. (1996). From participation to interaction: Toward the origins of interactive art. In L. Hershman Leeson (Ed.), *Clicking In: Hot links to a digital culture.* (pp.279-290). Seattle: Bay Press.

Donald, J. (1999). *Imagining the modern city.* Minneapolis: University of Minnesota Press.

Donath, J. (1997). Identity and deception in the virtual community. In P. Kollock, & M. Smith (Eds.), *Communities in cyberspace*. Berkeley: The University of California Press.

Duncum, P. (1991).Varieties of cultural literacy in art education. *Canadian Review of Art Education*, 18(1), 45-59.

Duncum, P. (1997). Coming to terms with consciousness in an age of electronic imagery. *Canadian Review of Art Education*, 23(1), 34-49.

Duncum, P. (1999a). Theorizing an art education of everyday aesthetics. *Canadian Review of Art Education*, 26(1) 44-56.

Duncum, P. (1999b). A case for an art education of everyday aesthetic experiences. *Studies in Art Education*, 40(4) 295-311.

Duncum, P. (2001).Visual culture: Developments, definitions, and directions for art education. *Studies in Art Education*, 42(2) 101-113.

Elkins, J. (2001). *Why art cannot be taught*. Urbana, IL: University of Illinois Press.

Farmer, J. (2000). *The new frontier: Art and television 1960-65.* Austin: Austin Museum of Art.

Feenberg, A. (2002). *Transforming technology: A critical theory revisited.* New York: Oxford University Press.

Felshin, N. (1995). Introduction. In N. Felshin (Ed.) *But is it art?* Seattle: Bay Press.

Fidler, R. (1997). *Mediamorphosis.* Thousand Oakes, CA: Pine Forge Press.

Foucault, M. (1971) *The order of things: An archaeology of the human sciences* (1st American edition). New York: Pantheon Books.

Foucault, M. (1984). Practices and sciences of the self. In P. Rabinow (Ed.). *Foucault reader* (pp. 331-390). New York: Pantheon books.

Foucault, M. (1988). Technologies of the self. In L. Martin, H. Gutman and P. Hutton (Eds.), *Technologies of the self: A seminar with Michel Foucault* (pp.16-49). Amherst: The University of Massachusetts Press.

Foucault, M. (1998). Of other spaces. In N. Mirzoeff (Ed.) *The visual culture reader*. New York: Routledge, pp. 237-244.

Franklin, U. (1999). *The real world of technology* (Revised Edition). Toronto: Anansi Press.

Freire, P. (1991). *Pedagogy of the city*. New York: Continuum.

Freedman, K. (2000). Social perspectives on art in the U.S.: Teaching visual culture in a democracy. *Studies in Art Education*, 41(4) 314-329.

Friedberg, A. (1995). *Window shopping: Cinema and the postmodern*. Berkeley: University of California Press.

Friedberg, A. (1998). The mobilized and virtual gaze in modernity: Flâneur/Flâneuse. In Mirzoeff, N. (Ed.) *The visual culture reader* (pp.253-262). New York: Routledge.

Frieling, R. (1996). Hot spots: Text in motion and the textscape of electronic media. In Hershman Leeson, L. (Ed.), *Clicking in: Hot links to a digital culture*. (pp.267-278).Seattle: Bay Press.

Gablik, S. (1991). *The reenchantment of art*. London: Thames and Hudson.

Gablik, S. (1995). *Conversations before the end of time*. London: Thames and Hudson.

Garoian, C. & Gaudelius, Y. (2001). Cyborg pedagogy: Performing in the digital age, *Studies in Art Education*. 42(4), 333-347.

Gigliotti, C. (2000). The ethical life of the digital aesthetic. In Lunenfeld, P. (Ed.) *The digital dialectic* (pp.46-63). Cambridge: MIT Press.

Götz, I. (2001). On person, technology, and education. *Educational Theory*, 51(1), 75-89.

Goodman, C. (1987). *Digital visions: Computers and art*. New York: Abrams.

Greene, M. (2000). *Releasing the imagination: Essays on education, the arts and social change*. San Francisco: Jossey Bass Publishers.

Griffins, T. (1997) Mass Production: Techne & Poesis. Retrieved 05/15/03 from http://tim.griffins.ca/writings/old/mass-production-techne-poesis.

Groden, M. & Kreiswirth, M. (1997) (Eds.) *The Johns Hopkins guide to literary theory and criticism.* The Johns Hopkins University press. retrieved from http://www.press.jhu.edu/books/hopkins_guide_to_literary_theory/entries/m._m._bakhtin.html January 6, 2004.

Grumet, M. (1981). Autobiography and reconceptualization. In Giroux, H. A., Penna, A. N., & Pinar, W. F. (Eds.), *Curriculum & instruction* (pp. 139-144). Berkely: McCutchan Publishing.

Grumet, M. (1981a). Show and tell: A response to the value issue in alternative paradigms for inquiry. In Guba, E. G. (Ed.) *The Paradigm Dialog.* Newbury Park, CA: Sage pp. 333-342.

Hall, S. (1996). *Who needs identity?* London: Sage Publications.

Haraway, D. (1991). *Simeons, Cyborgs, and women: The reinvention of nature.* New York: Routledge.

Haraway, D. (1993). A cyborg manifesto. In S. During (Ed.), *The cultural studies reader* (pp. 271-291). New York: Routledge.

Harvey, D. (1990). *The condition of postmodernity: An inquiry into the origins of social change.* Cambridge: Blackwell.

Harvey, D. (1993). From space to place and back again: Reflections on the condition of postmodernity. In J. Bird et al. (Eds.), *Mapping the futures: Local cultures, global change* (pp.3-29). London: Routledge.

Hayles, K. (1993). *Virtual bodies and flickering signifiers.* retrieved November 4, 2003 from: http://englishwww.humnet.ucla.edu/faculty/hatles/Flick.html

Heidegger, M. (1968). *What is called thinking?* New York: Harper & Row Publishers.

Heidegger, M. (1971). *Poetry, language, thought.* New York: Harper & Row Publishers.

Heidegger, M. (1977). *The Question concerning technology and other essays.* (W. Lovitt, Trans.). New York: Harper & Row Publishers.

Helfand, J. (2001*). Screen: Essays on graphic design, new media, and visual culture.* New York: Princeton Architectural Press.

Herivel, A. (1997). A voyage between tide and time: Creating research in the studio. *Canadian Review of Art Education*, 23(2) 55-73.

Hershman Leeson, L. (1996). Romancing the anti-body: Lust and longing in (Cyber)space. In Hershman Leeson, L. (Ed.), *Clicking in: Hot links to a digital culture.* (pp.325-337).Seattle: Bay Press.

Hicks, J. (1993). Technology and aesthetic education: A crucial synthesis. *Art Education, 46(6), 42-47.*

Huhtamo, E. (1996). Digitalian Treasures, or Glimpses of Art on the CD-ROM Frontier. In Hershman Leeson, L. (Ed.), *Clicking in: Hot links to a digital culture.* (pp.306-317).Seattle: Bay Press.

Jacob, E. (1987). Qualitative research traditions: A review. *Review of Educational Research,* 57(1), 1-50.

James, P. (1996). The construction of learning and teaching in a sculpture studio class. *Studies in Art education*, 37(3) 145-159.

Jameson, F. (2003). Fear and loathing in globalization. *New left review* (23)105-114.

Johnson, M. (1996). A comparative study of terms used in art education and computer graphics to describe the visual properties of images, *Studies in Art Education.* 37(3), 184-192.

Johnson, S. (1997). *Interface culture: How new technology transforms the way we create and communicate.* San Francisco: Harper Edge.

Jongeward, C. (1997). Visual portraits: Integrating artistic process into qualitative research. *Canadian Review of Art Education*, 24(2), 1-11.

Kearney, R. (1988). *The wake of the imagination*. London: Hutchinson.

Keifer-Boyd, K. (1996). Hypermedia and the Internet with critical inquiry in the arts: Preservice training. *Art Education*, 49(6), 33-41.

Kellner, D. (1989).Baudrillard: A new McLuhan? In D. Kellner (Ed.) *Illuminations* retrieved November 3, 2003 from: http://www.uta.edu/huma/illuminations/kell26.htm.

Krauss, R. (1993). *The optical unconscious*. Cambridge, MA: MIT Press.

Lalvani, S. (1996). *Photography, vision, and the production of modern bodies*. New York: State University of New York Press.

Landow, G. (2000). Hypertext as collage-writing. In Lunenfeld, P. (Ed.) *The digital dialectic* (pp.151-17). Cambridge: MIT Press.

Lanham, R. (1993). *The electronic word: Democracy, technology, and the arts*. Chicago: University of Chicago Press.

Lant, A. (1995). Haptical cinema. *October 74* (Fall 1995) 45-73.

Lankshear, C. & Knoeble, M. (2000). What is 'digital epistemologies'? retrieved September 18, 2003 from: http://www.edca.cqu.edu.au/~de/what.html

Lash, S. (2001). Technological forms of life. *Theory, culture & society*, 18(1) 105-120.

Lefevre, H. (1987). The everyday and everydayness. In S. Harris and D. Berke (Eds.), *Architecture of the everyday* (pp.32-37). New York: Princeton Architectural Press.

Lévy, P. (2001). *Cyberculture*. Translated by Robert Bononno, Minneapolis: University of Minnesota Press.

Logan, R. K. (2000). *The sixth language: Learning a living in the Internet age*. Stoddart: Toronto.

Lovejoy, M. (1997). *Postmodern currents: Art and artists in the age of electronic media*. New Jersey: Prentice Hall.

Manovich, L. (2001). *The language of new media*. Cambridge: The MIT Press.

Massey, D. (1994). *Space, place and gender*. Minneapolis: University of Minneapolis Press.

May, W. (1994). The Tie that binds: Reconstructing ourselves in institutional contexts. *Studies in Art Education*, 35 (3), 135-148.

McCarthy, A. (2001). *Ambient television: Visual culture and public space*. Durham: Duke University Press.

Mercedes, D. (1996). Digital ethics: Computers, photographs, and the manipulation of pixels. *Art Education*, 49(3), 44-50.

Miller, T. (1993). *The well tempered self.* Baltimore: The Johns Hopkins University Press.

Mirzoeff, N. (1998). What is visual culture? In Mirzoeff, N. (Ed.) *The visual culture reader* (pp.3-13). New York: Routledge.

Mirzoeff, N. (1999). *An introduction to visual culture*. New York: Routledge.

Morbey, M.L. (1993). Aaron: Portrait of the young machine as a male artist. *Revue d'art Canadienne/Canadian Art Review, XX,*_130-139.

Morbey, M.L. (1994). Implications of gendered technology for art education: The case study of a male drawing machine. *Arts and Learning Research: American Educational Research Association*, 10 (1), 88-100.

Morbey, M.L. (1995). Sorties into cyberspace: Art and electronic technologies. In L. Zuidervaart, & H. Luttikhuizen. (Eds.), *Pledges of jubilee: Essays on the arts and culture.* pp.56-77. Grand Rapids, MI: William B. Eernhartz.

Morgan, R. (1998). Media education in Ontario: Generational differences in approach. In A. Hart (Ed.). *Teaching the Media: International perspectives.* pp.145-167. New Jersey: Lawrence Erlbaum Associates, Publishers.

Morse, M. (1995). What do Cyborgs eat? Oral logic in an information society. In Bender, G. & Druckery, T. (Eds.) *Culture on the brink: Ideologies of technology*.(pp.157-189). second edition. Seattle: Bay Press.

Mulhall, S. (1996). *Heidegger and being and time*. London: Routledge.

Negroponte, N. (1995). *Being digital*. New York: Vintage Books.

Nietzsche, F. (1993). On Truth and lying in an extra-moral sense. In J. Rivkin, J.& M. Ryan (Eds). *Literary Theory: An Anthology*. Malden: Blackwell Publishers Inc. pp. 358-361.

Paterson, N. (1999). Technology / Art. *Fuse,* vol. 20, no. 5.

Paterson, M. (2000). *How the world touches us: Everyday embodied tactile - spatial experience.* Unpublished Departmental working paper for the

University of Bristol. Retrieved November 10, 2003 from: http://www.ggy.bris.ac.uk/postgraduates/ggmp/haptics/touches.htm

Pearse, H. (1992). Beyond paradigms: Art education theory and practice in a postparadigmatic world. *Studies in Art Education*, 33(4), 244-252.

Phillips, P. (1995). Maintenance activity: creating a climate for change. Felshin, N. (Ed.) *But is it art?* Seattle: Bay Press.

Probyn, E. (1990). Travels in the postmodern. In L. Nicholson (Ed.), *Feminism/Postmodernism* (pp.176-189). New York: Routledge.

Rabinow, P. (1984) (Ed.). *Foucault reader*. New York: Pantheon books.

Rheingold, H. (1993). *The virtual community: Homesteading on the electronic frontier*. Reading, MA: Addison-Wesley Publishing Co.

Rogers, P. (1995). Towards a language of computer art: When paint isn't paint. *Art Education*, 48(5), 17-22.

Roland, C. (1990). Our love affair with new technology: Is the Honeymoon over? *Art Education* 43(3), 54-60.

Rose, G. (1993). *Feminism and geography*. Cambridge: Polity Press.

Scott, J. (1992).Experience. In J. Butler and J. Scott (Eds.), *Feminists Theorize the Political.* New York: Routledge. pp.22-40.

Shields, R. (2000). Hypertext links: The ethic of the index and its space-time effects, in Herman, A. & Swiss, T. (Eds.), *The world wide web and contemporary cultural Theory* (pp.145-160). New York: Routledge.

Shohat, E. & Stam, R. (1998). Narrativizing visual culture: Towards a polycentric aesthetics. In Mirzoeff, N. (Ed.) *The visual culture reader* (pp.27-49). New York: Routledge.

Sofoulis, Z. (2001) Cyberquake: Haraway's Manifesto in *Cyberfeminismus: Feministische Visionen mit Netz und ohne Boden?* (issue of papers from eponymous seminars), Gabriele Jähnert, Karin Aleksander, Kersin Rosenbusch, eds., published as Bulletin Texte 24, Zentrum für interdisziplinäre Frauenforschung, Humboldt University, Berlin, pp. 54-72. Retrieved from: Nov. 12, 2003.

Stout, C. J. (1999).Artists as writers: Enriching perspectives in art appreciation. *Studies in Art Education*, 40(3), 226-241.

Sturken, M. & Cartwright, L. (2001). *Practices of looking*. New York: Oxford University Press.

Tapscott, D. (1998). *Growing up digital: The rise of the Net generation*. New York: McGraw-Hill.

Tomlinson, J. (1999). *Globalization and culture*. Chicago: The University of Chicago Press.

Trend, D. (1992). *Cultural pedagogy: Art, education, politics*. New York: Bergin & Garvey.

Trend, D. (1998). Introduction. In D. Trend (Ed.), *Reading digital culture* (pp.1-7). Oxford: Blackwell.

Tuan, Yi-Fu (2001). *Space and place: The perspective of experience*. Minneapolis: University of Minnesota Press.

Turkle, S. (1995). *Life on the screen*. New York: Touchstone Books.

Van Manen, M. (1982). Phenomenological pedagogy. *Curriculum inquiry*, 12(3), 283-299.

Varnedoe, K. & Gopnik, A. (1990). *High & low : Modern art and popular culture*. New York: The Museum of Modern Art.

Watrin, R. (1999). Art as research. *Canadian Review of Art Education*, 26(2) 92-100.

Williams, R. (1981). *Culture*. Glasgow: Fontana Paperbacks.

Williams, R. (1988). *Keywords, A vocabulary of culture and society*. London: Fontana Press.

Wolff, J. (1993). *The social production of art* (second edition). New York: New York University Press.

**INDEX**